THE COMPLETE ITALIAN COOKBOOK

THE COMPLETE ITALIAN COOKBOOK

INDEX

CONTENTS

Roast Sweet Potato Ravioli, page 67

Prosciutto-wrapped Pork with Polenta, page 126

Insalata Caprese, page 160

Frozen Zabaglione with Marsala Sauce, page 167

All recipes in this book have been double-tested.

When we test our recipes, we rate them for ease of preparation. The following cookery ratings are on the recipes in this book, making them easy to use and understand.

A single Cooking with Confidence symbol indicates a recipe that is simple and generally quick to make – perfect for beginners.

Two symbols indicate the need for just a little more care and a little more time.

Three symbols indicate special dishes that need more investment in time, care and patience—but the results are worth it.

NOTES
International conversions and a glossary containing unfamiliar terms can be found on page 208. Cooking times may vary slightly depending on the individual oven. We suggest you check the manufacturer's instructions to ensure proper temperature control.

THE TASTE OF ITALY

It is an understatement to say that food is important to the Italians. They love to eat, and meals are prepared with great pride and affection as a daily highlight of the family life which is central to their whole culture. The Italian style of cooking we know today developed from many isolated regional cuisines throughout the country. Though there were common threads, the geography, climate and outside influences of each region made them all unique. Pasta and risotto may have been known throughout Italy, but the ingredients which flavoured them varied, depending on which region you were dining in at the time. Generally, cheese and butter still feature prominently in northern Italy, reflecting the close proximity to the dairy-loving neighbours of Switzerland and Austria. Moving south, olive oil, tomatoes and fish define the Mediterranean diet.

Many regions boast a famous speciality, the production of which is a fiercely guarded tradition handed down through generations and sometimes even protected by law. Parmesan cheese is a good example of this. Although today there are very many varieties available, the best is widely accepted to be Parmigiano Reggiano, which comes from a strictly defined area around the city of Parma (also famous for its ham). Reggiano broadcasts its authenticity with its name emblazoned along the wide rind. The fact that many dishes are named for the city or region where they were first eaten, such as Spaghetti Napolitana (Naples) or Bolognese (Bologna), indicates the extent to which the Italians define themselves by their culinary heritage.

So where does this leave us today? Fortunate indeed, to be able to enjoy the best of all that Italy has to offer. Italian restaurants have been popular for many years and, despite a proliferation of questionable pizza and pasta joints, remain at the cutting edge of chic. And not just for special occasions—Italian food is now part of our day-to-day lives. We crunch biscotti with our morning caffe latte, grab a focaccia filled with mozzarella and prosciutto for lunch, and enjoy a bowl of spaghetti with pesto for dinner.

Cooking Italian food at home is an easy and enjoyable experience, with the vast majority of ingredients now

usually available at the supermarket and greengrocer.

The key to good Italian food is freshness. There are no second bests and no Italian cook would even contemplate preparing a dish without the best-quality, freshest ingredients. And if they aren't available, well then make something else instead. While pantry staples such as tinned tomatoes, anchovies, dried pasta, arborio rice and olive oil provide the backbone, fresh vegetables and herbs lift the dishes into the sublime. The Italian cook's favourite herbs are generally used fresh, often gathered from the surrounding area in great basketfuls. Basil is widely used to enhance tomato and pasta dishes and Italian parsley is the flat-leafed variety with a pungent aroma and flavour. Vegetables such as zucchini, eggplant, tomatoes, artichokes and capsicums are as delicious as they are good for you.

The 'Mediterranean' diet has been touted for many years as the healthy ideal, with olive oil now being revered rather than reviled. Fortunately, it is not so worthy as to be dull and unappetizing, but consists of dishes which combine those two truly mouth-watering ingredients—health and happiness.

Although today we have become accustomed to pizza or pasta as a full meal in itself, the Italian dinner in its glorious entirety is a true work of art. The opening spread is the antipasto, meaning 'before the meal', intended not to satisfy but merely titillate the palate. An antipasto platter can be an elaborate array of marinated seafood, aromatic salads and frittata, or a simple plate of prosciutto with ripe figs and juicy melon slices. The only golden rule, as always, is that freshness abounds. To follow, come the primi piatti or 'first plates'. These can vary endlessly, but will more often than not consist of a hearty Italian soup (Minestrone being by far the best known) or pasta, polenta or risotto. We are, on the whole, unused to filling up on starch or carbohydrate before the main dish, but as a tradition in a country where meat may have been scarce or costly, it makes great sense. It also goes to explain the wonderful simplicity of Italian meat or fish dishes.

Vegetarians and non-red-meat eaters fare well with Italian cuisine. Staples such as polenta, rice and pasta are filling and satisfying and, when dressed up with beans, seafood and fresh vegetables, provide great nutrition. The vast majority of Italian meals are finished off with a simple piece of fresh fruit, but to balance all this healthiness, the Italians have also let their national sweet tooth run riot and devised a vast array of wicked desserts, cakes and biscuits. Their gelato and other ice confections, such as Granita and Cassata, are world-renowned. Admittedly, Tiramisu may have been done to death in all the fashionable restaurants around town, but who cares? Like all Italian food, it still tastes wonderful.

GLOSSARY OF INGREDIENTS

Most of the ingredients for Italian cooking are well-known to us, but there are a few which have come into vogue only in the last few years. The majority are available in the supermarket or you may have to make a trip to the delicatessen. The golden rule is to always buy the best quality you can afford.

ANCHOVIES
A small fish from the herring family with slightly oily flesh and a strong flavour. Anchovies can be eaten fresh, although they are rarely found outside Mediterranean fishing ports as the fish are delicate and need to be eaten or processed quickly. They are widely available as salted fillets marinated in oil, sold in jars or cans.

ARBORIO RICE
Arborio rice derives its name from a small village in the Piedmont region in northern Italy where it is grown. It has a short, pearly grain and is used in both sweet and savoury dishes. Arborio rice is particularly suited to making risotto—the rice absorbs a large amount of cooking liquid and becomes tender and creamy but not too soft.

ARTICHOKE HEARTS
The fleshy centres or 'hearts' of the thistly artichoke head. These are available whole or quartered, canned or in jars, in marinade or brine.

BALSAMIC VINEGAR
A richly flavoured, dark-coloured vinegar. This has a bitter-sweet taste, a slightly syrupy consistency and is used in salad dressings, sauces or as a meat marinade. Balsamic vinegar is made in Modena, Italy, from unfermented Trebbiano (white) grapes. It is aged in wooden casks for no less than five years and sometimes up to a hundred. Price and quality vary greatly and are dependent on the age.

BOCCONCINI
Traditionally shaped in balls, like a smaller version of Mozzarella cheese and often referred to as 'baby mozzarella'. Originally made in southern Italy from water buffalo milk, but now made using cows milk. This fresh, unripened cheese takes 24 hours to make, is milky white, soft and has a slightly sweet flavour. To keep it moist, it should be stored in the whey in which it is sold.

BORLOTTI BEAN
A slightly kidney-shaped bean which is a pale, pinky brown colour with darker speckled markings. It has a smooth texture and a ham-like flavour when cooked and is used in soups, stews, casseroles or salads. Available dried, canned or fresh in season.

CANNELLINI BEAN
A white, slightly kidney-shaped bean, also known as Italian haricot bean or white kidney bean. Mildly flavoured and slightly fluffy in texture when cooked, these are good all-purpose beans for use in soups, casseroles, stews and salads. Available dried or canned.

CAPERS
The unopened, olive-green flower buds of a prickly shrub native to the Mediterranean, the Middle East and northern Africa. These are sold in a seasoned vinegar or packed in salt. Capers have a sharp sour taste and are used in sauces, salad dressings and often as an accompaniment to smoked salmon. Salted capers should be washed thoroughly before use.

FONTINA
Prized by connoisseurs as being among the six greatest cheeses of the world. Fontina is a semi-hard flat round cheese with a smooth creamy texture and slightly sweet nutty flavour. Traditionally served in Italian dishes, melted over polenta.

GNOCCHI
Small soft Italian dumplings made from semolina or potato dough and sometimes flavoured with spinach, pumpkin or cheese. Not to be confused with the dried pasta of the same name.

MASCARPONE
A fresh unripened soft cream cheese with a slightly sour flavour, originally from Lombardy. It can be eaten fresh with fruit, and is widely used in Italian cooking, usually in desserts and cheesecakes.

MOZZARELLA

A smooth white cheese with a mild, slightly sweet flavour. Often eaten fresh in Italy, in a simple salad with tomatoes and olives, but best known for its use on pizzas.

OLIVE OIL

A pale yellow to deep green, mono-unsaturated oil made from pressed olives. It has a fruity flavour and is used for frying and in salad dressings.

Extra virgin olive oil is a cold pressed oil from the first pressing of the olives. It has a strong flavour and is deep green in colour.

Virgin olive oil is from the second pressing of the olives and is slightly milder in flavour and a little lighter in colour.

Light olive oil is made from subsequent pressings and has usually been heated in the extraction process. The flavour is very mild and it is light in colour—not lower in fat, as is sometimes assumed from the name.

PANCETTA

Unsmoked bacon, from the belly of the pig, that has been cured with spices. It is usually sold rolled into a sausage shape and cut into very thin slices.

PARMESAN

A very hard cows milk cheese with a strong sharp taste and grainy texture. Widely used in Italian cooking, either grated in dishes or as shavings to garnish. Always buy Parmesan in a chunk from a delicatessen and grate it as you need it rather than using the ready grated packet Parmesan. The variety which is stamped 'Parmigiano Reggiano' on the rind is the most superior Parmesan—this is, of course, reflected in the price, but it is worth it.

PECORINO

A cooked curd sheeps milk cheese, available in two varieties: Romano, a hard grating cheese similar to Parmesan, and Fresco, a young, softer version that can be served as a table cheese.

PINE NUTS

The small, slender, soft golden seed shed by the fully mature cone of certain types of pine tree. Traditionally used for stuffings, salads, cakes and biscuits, but best known as a key ingredient in pesto sauce.

POLENTA

Polenta is another name for cornmeal, and is also the name of the dish made from the cornmeal. The dish is a thick porridge which is eaten with casseroles and stews or, with the addition of Parmesan cheese, is left to set firm and then grilled or fried.

PROSCIUTTO

A cured Italian ham taken from the hind of the pig. Aged for eight to ten months, it is sliced wafer thin and may be cooked or served raw. Prosciutto di Parma is the classic Italian ham, produced from pigs fattened on the whey left over from making the local cheese, Parmigiano Reggiano.

RADICCHIO

A deep purple, lettuce-like vegetable with a sharp, bitter flavour. Used in salads or braised or grilled and served with meat or chicken.

RICOTTA

A soft, moist white cheese with a slightly sweet flavour. Used in savoury spreads, or as a dessert with fruit or as a filling for cheesecakes.

ROCKET

A salad green with slender deep green leaves. This has a peppery, bitter flavour that complements other leaves in a mixed green salad. The older and larger the leaf, the stronger its flavour.

Romano

A hard grating cheese usually made from cows milk, this has a similar texture and taste to Parmesan. When made with sheeps milk it is called Pecorino Romano.

SUN-DRIED TOMATOES

Widely available either dry and loosely packed or in jars in oil. The dry variety need to be rehydrated before use—cover with boiling water and leave for about 10 minutes. If buying sun-dried tomatoes in oil, choose the variety in olive oil—you can then use this for cooking as it will have extra flavour.

DRIED PASTA

Dried pasta is commercially prepared and packaged, made from flour, water,
and salt and sometimes egg. Some shapes are especially suited to a particular type
of sauce. Here we have given a guide to suitable sauces but you do not have to stick
to any strict rules—it's your choice.

*Below: Tagliatelle
(best with thin
coating sauces)*

*Right: Tomato tagliatelle
(excellent with thin
coating sauces)*

*Left: Penne
(best with thick
or chunky sauces)*

*Left: Rigatoni
(best with
chunky or
thick sauces)*

*Right: Lasagne
(layered with
sauces and baked)*

*Below: Conchiglie or
shells (best with chunky
sauces which get trapped
in shells)*

*Above: Fettuccine
(excellent with thin
coating sauces)*

*Left: Risoni (added to
soups, casseroles)*

Left: Linguine (best with thin coating sauces)

Left: Fusilli (best with sauces which get trapped in grooves)

Left: Orecchiette (best with sauces which get trapped in grooves)

Right: Spaghetti (best with thin coating sauces or bolognaise)

Above: Spiral pasta (best with sauces which get trapped in grooves)

Left: Spinach tagliatelle (best with thin coating sauces)

Below: Macaroni (best in baked dishes, soups)

Above: Farfalle or butterflies (best with sauces which get trapped in grooves)

Above: Tortellini shapes (excellent with sauces which get trapped in grooves)

Above: Cannelloni (stuffed with filling and baked in a sauce)

Above: Ziti (suitable for thick or thin sauces)

Above right: Miniature star-shaped pasta (best for soups)

Above: Macaroni elbows (best in baked dishes, soups)

11

FRESH PASTA

Specialty pasta shops and some supermarkets and delicatessens stock fresh pasta. Some are flavoured with herbs and spices or coloured with vegetables. Fresh pasta cooks a lot more quickly than dried pasta. Here we have suggested types of sauces for each pasta.

Right: Lasagne sheets (layered with thick sauces and baked)

Above: Ravioli (excellent with mildflavoured thin sauces)
Below: Pumpkin Gnocchi (best with thin sauces)

Left: Tortellini (best with mild-flavoured thin sauces)

Below: Gnocchi (excellent with thin sauces)

Left: Cracked pepper tagliatelle (best with thin coating sauces)

Below right: Spinach gnocchi
(best with thin coating sauces)

Below: Pumpkin ravioli
(best with mild-
flavoured thin sauces)

Below right: Tomato tagliatelle
Below left: Spinach tagliatelle
(both are best with thin
coating sauces)

Left: Spaghetti (best with thin
coating sauces or bolognaise)

Above: Spinach tortellini
(excellent with thin sauces)

Above: Pappardelle
(suitable for thick, thin
or chunky sauces)

13

CLASSIC PASTA SAUCES

BOLOGNESE

1 Heat 2 tablespoons oil in a large pan and add 1 onion, 1 carrot and 1 celery stick, all diced. Cook over low heat for 10 minutes, stirring occasionally.

2 Add 2 crushed cloves of garlic and cook for 1 more minute. Increase the heat slightly, add 500 g (1 lb) of beef mince and cook until well browned. Break up any lumps of meat with a fork as it cooks.

3 Pour in 2 cups (500 ml/ 16 fl oz) beef stock, 1½ cups (375 ml/12 fl oz) red wine, two 425 g (13½ oz) cans crushed peeled tomatoes, 2 tablespoons chopped fresh parsley and 2 teaspoons sugar.

4 Bring to the boil, then reduce the heat and simmer uncovered for 1½ hours, stirring occasionally, until reduced and thickened. Season to taste and serve over spaghetti. Serves 4.

POMODORO

1 Take 500 g (1 lb) ripe tomatoes and score a small cross in the base of each. Place in a large heatproof bowl and cover with boiling water. Leave for 2 minutes.

2 Drain the tomatoes and allow to cool slightly. Peel the skin away from the cross and discard. Cut the tomatoes in half and scoop out the seeds with a teaspoon. Roughly chop the tomato flesh.

3 Heat 2 tablespoons oil in a large pan and add 1 large chopped onion. Cook over low heat for 15 minutes, stirring occasionally, until very soft. Add 2 crushed cloves of garlic and cook for a further 2 minutes.

4 Add the tomato flesh, 2 teaspoons sugar and salt and pepper to taste. Cook uncovered over a low heat for 20 minutes, stirring occasionally. Cool slightly and purée in a blender or food processor. Reheat and serve with penne. Serves 4.

CARBONARA

1 Remove and discard the rind from 8 rashers of bacon. Cut the bacon into thin strips. Place in a frying pan and cook over medium heat until brown and crisp.

2 Cook 500 g (1 lb) of spaghetti in a large pan of boiling water until tender. Drain well in a colander and then return to the pan.

3 Beat 4 eggs, 1¼ cups (315 ml/10 fl oz) cream and ½ cup (50 g/1⅔ oz) freshly grated Parmesan cheese together. Add the bacon to the pasta and pour in the egg mixture.

4 Toss well to combine the ingredients. Return to very low heat and toss for about 30 seconds–1 minute, until the sauce has cooked and slightly thickened. Serve immediately. Serves 4.

PESTO

1 Place ¼ cup (40 g/1⅓ oz) pine nuts in a frying pan, and cook, stirring, over low heat for a couple of minutes until golden. Transfer to a plate to cool.

2 Put 2 firmly packed cups (100 g/3⅓ oz) whole fresh basil leaves into a food processor. Crush 2 cloves of garlic and add to the basil.

3 Finely grate 25 g (¾ oz) Parmesan cheese and add to the processor along with the toasted pine nuts. Process until finely chopped.

4 With the motor running, add ½ cup (125 ml/4 fl oz) extra virgin olive oil in a slow stream. Process until all the oil has been added and the mixture is a thick, slightly runny paste. Serve over fettucine. Serves 4.

CLASSIC PASTA SAUCES

PUTTANESCA

1 Heat 2 tablespoons oil in a large pan, add 3 anchovy fillets and cook, stirring, for a couple of minutes, until the anchovies break up.

2 Add 3 crushed cloves of garlic and ½ teaspoon chilli flakes to the pan. Stir-fry for a further minute, taking care not to burn the garlic or it will become bitter.

3 Add two 425 g (13½ oz) cans crushed tomatoes and bring to the boil. Reduce the heat to simmer, uncovered, for 20 minutes, or until the sauce has reduced and thickened.

4 Stir in 2 tablespoons capers, ¼ cup (35 g/1¼ oz) chopped black olives and 2 teaspoons chopped fresh oregano leaves. Cook for a further 10 minutes. Serve over spaghetti. Serves 4.

BOSCAIOLA

1 Wipe 500 g (1 lb) button mushrooms with a damp paper towel to remove any dirt. Slice the mushrooms finely, stems included.

2 Heat 2 tablespoons oil in a large pan; add 1 chopped onion. Cook over medium heat for about 5 minutes, or until golden. Add 2 crushed cloves of garlic and cook for 1 minute further.

3 Add the mushrooms and 425 g (13½ oz) can crushed tomatoes to the pan; bring to the boil. Reduce the heat, cover and leave to simmer for 15 minutes.

4 Stir in 2 tablespoons chopped flat-leaf parsley. Toss a little sauce through 500 g (1 lb) cooked fusilli and serve topped with the remaining sauce. Serves 4.

AMATRICIANA

1 Take 500 g (1 lb) ripe tomatoes and score a small cross in the base of each. Place in a large heatproof bowl and cover with boiling water. Leave for 2 minutes.

2 Drain the tomatoes and allow to cool slightly. Peel the skin away from the cross and discard. Roughly chop the tomato flesh.

3 Heat 30 g (1 oz) butter in a large frying pan, add a finely chopped onion and cook for 5 minutes over medium low heat, until soft and golden. Cut 6 thin slices of pancetta into small strips, and add to the onion. Cook for 2 minutes to brown.

4 Add the tomatoes to the pan, along with 2 teaspoons of very finely chopped red chilli. Bring to the boil, reduce the heat and simmer uncovered for 20 minutes, stirring occasionally. Serve on bucatini. Serves 4.

PRIMAVERA

1 Trim the ends from 155 g (5 oz) of asparagus spears and cut into 1 cm (½ inch) lengths. Place in a heatproof bowl and cover with boiling water. Leave for 1 minute, drain and cool.

2 Melt 40 g (1⅓ oz) butter in a large pan, add 1 small onion, 1 small zucchini and 1 small carrot, all diced, and cook over moderate heat for about 7 minutes, until soft, stirring occasionally.

3 Add the asparagus to the pan, and cook for 1 minute. Add ½ cup (125 ml/4 fl oz) cream, stir and then warm through. Season with salt and pepper to taste.

4 Add 500 g (1 lb) cooked fettucine to the vegetable mixture with 30 g (1 oz) grated Parmesan cheese. Toss together, then serve immediately. Serves 4.

ANTIPASTI

BRUSCHETTA WITH MEDITERRANEAN TOPPINGS

Preparation time: 20 minutes
Total cooking time: 15 minutes
Serves 4–6

CAPSICUM TOPPING
1 yellow capsicum
1 red capsicum
1 green capsicum

TOMATO AND BASIL TOPPING
2 ripe tomatoes
¼ cup (15 g/½ oz) shredded fresh
   basil
1 tablespoon extra virgin
   olive oil

12 slices crusty Italian bread
2 cloves garlic, halved
⅓ cup (80 ml/2¾ fl oz) extra virgin
   olive oil
1 tablespoon chopped flat-leaf parsley

1 To make Capsicum Topping: Cut the capsicums in half lengthways and remove the seeds and membrane. Flatten slightly and place, skin-side-up, under a hot grill until the skins are blackened. Cover with a tea towel or put the capsicums in a paper or plastic bag, seal and leave until cool. Peel away the skins and discard. Slice the flesh into strips.
2 To make Tomato and Basil Topping: Finely chop the tomatoes and combine in a bowl with the basil and olive oil. Season with freshly ground black pepper.
3 To make Bruschetta: Toast the bread slices and, while still hot, rub with the cut side of a garlic clove. Drizzle olive oil over each slice of bread and sprinkle with salt and plenty of freshly ground black pepper.
4 Arrange the Capsicum Topping on top of half the bread slices; sprinkle with parsley. Arrange the Tomato and Basil Topping on the remaining slices of bread. Serve immediately.

COOK'S FILE
Note: Extra virgin olive oil is produced from the first pressing of the olives. Using a superior oil in your cooking makes the difference between a good dish and a great one—always use the best-quality oil you can afford. 'Light' olive oil is from the last pressing and has a very mild flavour.

Grill the capsicums until the skin is blackened, leave to cool, then peel.

Rub the hot toasted bruschetta with the cut side of the garlic clove.

BRUSCHETTA SELECTION

To make basic bruschetta, cut a crusty Italian loaf into twelve 1.5 cm diagonal slices. Toast or grill the slices until golden. Bruise 2 garlic cloves with the flat of a knife, peel and rub the cloves over both sides of the hot bread. Drizzle the tops with a little extra virgin olive oil and finish with one of these delicious toppings.

ANCHOVY, TOMATO AND OREGANO

Deseed and roughly chop 3 vine-ripened tomatoes and mix with 1 small chopped red onion, a 90 g jar drained, minced anchovy fillets and 2 tablespoons olive oil. Spoon some of the mixture onto each bruschetta. Drizzle with extra virgin olive oil, and garnish with chopped fresh oregano and freshly ground black pepper.

BLACK OLIVE PATÉ, ROCKET AND FETA

Place 100 g trimmed baby rocket leaves, 75 g crumbled Greek feta and 2 tablespoons olive oil in a bowl, and mix together well. Spread 2 teaspoons of black olive pâté onto each bruschetta slice and top with the feta mixture. Drizzle with extra virgin olive oil and season with sea salt and freshly ground black pepper.

SUN-DRIED TOMATO PESTO, ARTICHOKE AND BOCCONCINI

Spread 1 teaspoon of good-quality sun-dried tomato pesto onto each slice of bruschetta. Slice 12 (360 g) bocconcini and place on top of the pesto. Chop 55 g drained marinated artichoke hearts in oil and place over the bocconcini slices. Sprinkle with some finely chopped fresh flat-leaf parsley.

PESTO, RED CAPSICUM AND PARMESAN

Cut 3 medium red capsicums into large flattish pieces and remove the seeds and membrane. Cook the capsicum pieces, skin-side-up, under a hot grill until the skin blackens and blisters. Place in a plastic bag and leave to cool. When cool enough to handle, peel away the skin. Discard the skin and cut the flesh into 1 cm strips. Spread 2 teaspoons good-quality basil pesto onto each slice of the bruschetta. Top with the red capsicum strips and 50 g fresh Parmesan shards. Drizzle with extra virgin olive oil and season with sea salt and freshly ground black pepper.

MUSHROOM AND GOAT CHEESE

Preheat the oven to moderate 180°C (350°F/Gas 4). Mix ½ cup (125 ml) olive oil with 3 chopped garlic cloves, 2 tablespoons chopped fresh flat-leaf parsley and 1 tablespoon dry sherry. Place 6 large field mushrooms on a foil-lined baking tray and spoon on all but 2 tablespoons of the mixture. Bake for 20 minutes, or until soft. Mix 150 g goat cheese with 1 teaspoon chopped fresh thyme, then spread over the bruschetta. Warm the remaining oil mixture. Cut the mushrooms in half and place one half on each bruschetta. Drizzle with the remaining oil. Season with sea salt and ground black pepper.

PAN CON TOMATE

Place 4 seeded and roughly chopped large vine-ripened tomatoes, ½ cup (15 g) torn fresh basil leaves, 2 tablespoons olive oil and ½ teaspoon caster sugar in a bowl and mix well. Season wth plenty of sea salt and freshly ground black pepper and set the mixture aside for 10–15 minutes so the flavours have time to infuse and develop. Cut a ripe vine-ripened tomato in half and rub it on the oiled side of the slices of bruschetta, squeezing the tomato to extract as much of the liquid as possible. Carefully spoon 2 tablespoons of the tomato mixture onto each slice of bruschetta and serve immediately.

Left to right: Anchovy, Tomato and Oregano Bruschetta; Black Olive Pâté, Rocket and Feta Bruschetta; Sun-dried Tomato Pesto, Artichoke and Bocconcini Bruschetta; Pesto, Red Capsicum and Parmesan Bruschetta; Mushroom and Goat Cheese Bruschetta; Pan con Tomate.

ANTIPASTO

What more delicious way to whet the appetite than with a colourful antipasto platter? The name translates literally as 'before the meal' and the tradition arose from the lengthy banquets of the Roman Empire. These recipes serve 4–8 people, depending on how many dishes you prepare.

CANNELLINI BEAN SALAD

Rinse and drain a 425 g (13½ oz) can cannellini beans and toss together with 1 tablespoon finely chopped red onion, 1 chopped tomato, 3 sliced anchovy fillets, 2 teaspoons finely chopped basil leaves, 2 teaspoons extra virgin olive oil and 1 teaspoon balsamic vinegar. Season to taste.

ARTICHOKE FRITTATA

Heat 30 g (1 oz) butter in a non-stick frying pan, add 2 small sliced leeks and 1 sliced clove of garlic and cook until soft. Spread evenly over the bottom of the pan. Lightly beat 6 eggs and season with salt and black pepper. Slice 100 g (3⅓ oz) bottled artichoke hearts. Pour the eggs into the pan and arrange the artichoke slices on top. Sprinkle with 1 teaspoon chopped fresh tarragon. Cook over low heat until set (this will take about 10 minutes), shaking the pan occasionally to evenly distribute the egg. Place under a hot grill to lightly brown the top. Cut into wedges and drizzle with a little lemon juice to serve.

Clockwise from left: Cannellini Bean Salad; Artichoke Frittata; Ricotta Spread; Italian Meatballs; Marinated Mushrooms.

RICOTTA SPREAD

Beat 200 g (6½ oz) ricotta with 2 tablespoons lemon juice until smooth and then fold in 3 tablespoons sliced black olives and 1 tablespoon chopped sun-dried tomatoes. Pile into a serving bowl and sprinkle with 1 tablespoon chopped chives. Serve with crusty Italian bread.

ITALIAN MEATBALLS

Combine 250 g (8 oz) lean beef mince, a grated small onion, 1 crushed clove of garlic, ½ cup (40 g/1⅓ oz) fresh white breadcrumbs, 3 tablespoons chopped black olives, 1 teaspoon dried oregano, 1 tablespoon finely chopped parsley and salt and black pepper to taste. Mix together thoroughly with your hands. Form teaspoonsful of mixture into balls. Heat a little oil in a frying pan and cook the meatballs in batches until well browned.

MARINATED MUSHROOMS

Wipe 315 g (10 oz) small button mushrooms clean with damp paper towels and cut in half (never wash mushrooms by soaking them in water or they will become soggy). Place the mushrooms in a bowl with 3 finely sliced spring onions and 1 finely sliced celery stick, then gently mix together. Stir through 1 crushed clove of garlic, 3 tablespoons extra virgin olive oil, 2 tablespoons lemon juice and 1 tablespoon finely chopped chives. Refrigerate for about 4 hours for the flavours to combine, but allow to return to room temperature before serving.

Note: For a delicious mushroom salad, use the same recipe for Marinated Mushrooms but place the mushrooms in the base of a large salad bowl. Top with torn lettuce leaves or a mixture of torn salad leaves and toss well just before serving. You may need to make more dressing (marinade), depending on the amount of lettuce in your salad.

CARPACCIO

Take a 400 g (12⅔ oz) piece of beef eye fillet
and remove all the visible fat and sinew. Freeze
for 1–2 hours, until firm but not frozen solid
(this makes the meat easier to slice thinly). Cut
paper thin slices of beef with a large, sharp knife.
Arrange on a serving platter and allow to return
to room temperature. Drizzle with 1 tablespoon
extra virgin olive oil, then scatter with torn rocket
leaves, black olives cut into slivers and shavings
of Parmesan cheese. Serve at room temperature.

PASTA FRITTATA

Cook 300 g (9⅔ oz) spaghetti in a large pan of boiling
water, until just tender but still retaining a little bite, then
drain well. Whisk 4 eggs together in a large bowl, then
add ½ cup (50 g/1⅔ oz) finely grated Parmesan cheese,
2 tablespoons chopped fresh parsley and salt and freshly
ground black pepper. Add the spaghetti and toss together
until well coated. Melt 1 tablespoon butter in a large
frying pan and add the spaghetti mixture. Cover and cook
over low heat until the base is crisp and golden. Slide the
frittata onto a plate, melt another tablespoon of butter in
the pan and flip the frittata back in to cook the other side
(do not cover or the Frittata will not get a crisp finish).
Serve warm, cut into wedges.

STUFFED CHERRY TOMATOES

Slice the tops from 16 cherry tomatoes, hollow out and discard the seeds. Turn upside-down and leave to drain for a few minutes. Beat together 50 g (1⅔ oz) each goats cheese and ricotta until smooth. Finely chop 2 slices prosciutto, discarding any fat, and mix with the cheeses. Season with salt and ground black pepper. Stuff into the tomatoes, using your fingers, and refrigerate until required.

PROSCIUTTO WITH MELON

Cut a melon (rockmelon or honeydew) into thin wedges and remove the seeds. Wrap a slice of prosciutto around each piece of fruit, drizzle with a little extra virgin olive oil and grind some black pepper over each.

From left: Carpaccio; Pasta frittata; Stuffed cherry tomatoes; Prosciutto with Melon; Marinated Eggplant.

MARINATED EGGPLANT

Cut 750 g (1½ lb) slender eggplant into thick diagonal slices. Put in a colander and sprinkle well with salt. After 30 minutes, rinse and pat dry. Mix 3 tablespoons olive oil, 2 tablespoons balsamic vinegar, 2 crushed cloves of garlic and 1 finely chopped anchovy fillet; whisk until smooth and season to taste. Heat a little oil in a large non-stick frying pan and brown the eggplant on both sides. Place in a bowl, add the dressing and 2 tablespoons chopped parsley and toss. Marinate for 4 hours and serve at room temperature.

25

SEAFOOD ANTIPASTO

A speciality of coastal areas of Italy, a selection of seafood antipasto makes an especially delicious start to a meal.

CHAR-GRILLED OCTOPUS

Combine ⅔ cup (170 ml/5½ fl oz) olive oil, ⅓ cup (10 g/ ⅓ oz) chopped fresh oregano, ⅓ cup (10 g/⅓ oz) chopped fresh parsley, 3 finely chopped small red chillies and 3 cloves of crushed garlic in a large bowl. Wash 1 kg (2 lb) baby octopus and dry well. Slit the head open and remove the gut. Grasp the body firmly and push the beak out with your index finger. Add the octopus to the oil mixture and marinate for 3–4 hours or overnight. Drain, reserving the marinade. Cook on a very hot barbecue or in a very hot pan for 3–5 minutes, or until the flesh turns white. Turn frequently and brush with the marinade during cooking.

SCALLOP FRITTERS

Combine 6 lightly beaten eggs with ¼ cup (25 g/¾ oz) grated Parmesan, 3 cloves crushed garlic, 1 cup (125 g/4 oz) plain flour and 2 tablespoons each chopped fresh thyme and oregano. Mix well with a wooden spoon until smooth. Fold in 250 g (8 oz) cleaned and chopped scallops. Heat oil for shallow-frying until moderately hot. Pour quarter-cupfuls of batter into the hot oil and cook in batches for 4–5 minutes over moderate heat, until golden brown. Drain on paper towels and serve with mayonnaise or plain yoghurt.

SARDINES IN VINE LEAVES

Place 12 fresh vine leaves in a large heatproof bowl and cover with boiling water. Leave for 2–3 minutes, rinse with cold water, drain and pat dry. If using vine leaves in brine, soak in cold water for 30 minutes, drain and pat dry. Preheat the oven to moderate 180°C (350°F/Gas 4). Heat 1 tablespoon olive oil in a frying pan and add 1 crushed clove of garlic, 1 finely chopped spring onion and 2 tablespoons pine nuts. Cook, stirring, until the pine nuts just begin to turn brown. Combine in a bowl with 3 tablespoons chopped parsley, 2 teaspoons finely grated lemon rind and 3 tablespoons fresh white breadcrumbs. Season with salt and freshly ground black pepper. Fill 12 sardine fillets with the breadcrumb mixture and wrap each in a vine leaf. Place in a single layer in a well greased baking dish. Drizzle with 2 tablespoons olive oil and bake for 30 minutes. Serve at room temperature, with mayonnaise flavoured with crushed garlic.

From left: Char-grilled Octopus; Scallop Fritters; Sardines in Vine Leaves; Marinated Seafood; Smoked Cod Frittata with Rocket; Mussels with Crispy Prosciutto.

MUSSELS WITH CRISPY PROSCIUTTO

Heat 1 tablespoon oil in a small frying pan. Add 1 finely chopped onion, 6 thin slices prosciutto, chopped, and 4 crushed cloves garlic. Cook until the prosciutto is crispy and the onion softened, then set aside. Add 1.5 kg (3 lb) cleaned mussels to a large pot of boiling water and cook for 5 minutes, discarding any that don't open. Remove the mussels from their shells, keeping half of each shell. Place two mussels on each half-shell and top with the prosciutto mixture. Combine ½ cup (50 g/1⅔ oz) grated Parmesan and ½ cup (60 g/2 oz) grated Cheddar cheese and sprinkle over the prosciutto. Cook under a preheated grill until the cheese has melted and the mussels are warmed through.

SMOKED COD FRITTATA WITH ROCKET

Place 500 g (1 lb) smoked cod in a pan with enough milk and water to cover. Bring to the boil, then reduce the heat and simmer for 3–4 minutes. Remove with a slotted spoon and flake the flesh. Whisk 8 eggs in a bowl. Add ½ cup (50 g/1⅔ oz) grated Parmesan and ½ cup (60 g/2 oz) grated Cheddar cheese, 2 tablespoons chopped fresh thyme, ½ cup (30 g/1 oz) torn basil leaves and the fish. Mix to combine. Heat 2 tablespoons olive oil in a large heavy-based frying pan. Pour in the mixture and cook over medium heat for 5 minutes, or until nearly cooked. Place under a hot grill for 3–4 minutes, or until just set and lightly golden. Transfer to a large serving platter and pile 2 cups (40 g/1⅓ oz) torn rocket leaves in the centre.

MARINATED SEAFOOD

Slice 500 g (1 lb) small squid hoods into rings. Shell and devein 500 g (1 lb) raw prawns. Scrub and remove the beards from 500 g (1 lb) mussels, discarding any which are already open. Put 3 cups (750 ml/24 fl oz) water, ½ cup (125 ml/4 fl oz) white wine vinegar, ½ teaspoon of salt and 3 bay leaves in a large pan and bring to the boil. Add the squid and 500 g (1 lb) scallops, then reduce the heat to low and simmer for 2–3 minutes, or until the seafood has turned white. Remove squid and scallops with a slotted spoon and place in a bowl. Repeat the process with the prawns, cooking until just pink. Return the liquid to the boil then add the mussels; cover, reduce the heat and simmer for about 3 minutes, until all the shells are open. Discard any mussels that don't open. Cool the mussels, remove the meat and add to the bowl. Whisk together 2 crushed cloves of garlic, ½ cup (125 ml/4 fl oz) extra virgin olive oil, 3 tablespoons lemon juice, 1 tablespoon white wine vinegar, 1 teaspoon Dijon mustard and 1 table-spoon chopped parsley. Pour over seafood and toss well. Refrigerate for 1–2 hours; serve on a bed of lettuce leaves.

Note: Any seafood can be used for this dish—the most important thing to remember is that seafood should never be overcooked or it will become tough. To make this dish more economical, substitute white fish fillets for most of the prawns and scallops. Poach the fish in the cooking liquid for a few minutes, drain immediately and cut into chunks. Toss carefully with the rest of the seafood in the dressing and garnish with a few cooked prawns and scallops.

BAKED RICOTTA AND RED CAPSICUM WITH PESTO

Preparation time: 10 minutes
Total cooking time: 45 minutes
Serves 6

1 large red capsicum, cut into
   quarters and seeded
750 g ricotta
1 egg
6 slices wholegrain bread

PESTO
2 tablesoons pine nuts
2 cups (100 g) fresh basil
2 cloves garlic
2 tablespoons good-quality olive oil
2 tablespoons finely grated fresh
   Parmesan

1 Grill the capsicum, skin-side up, under a hot grill for 5–6 minutes, or until the skin blackens and blisters. Place in a bowl and cover with plastic wrap until cool enough to handle. Peel off the skin and slice the flesh into 2 cm wide strips.

2 To make the Pesto, place the pine nuts, basil and garlic in a food processor and process for 15 seconds, or until finely chopped. While the processor is running add the oil in a continuous thin stream, then season with salt and freshly ground black pepper. Stir in the Parmesan.

3 Preheat the oven to moderate 180°C (350°F/Gas 4). Grease six texas muffin holes.

4 Mix the ricotta and egg until well combined. Season with salt and freshly ground black pepper. Divide the capsicum strips among the muffin holes, top with 2 teaspoons Pesto and spoon in the ricotta mixture.

5 Bake for 35–40 minutes, or until the ricotta is firm and golden. Cool, then unmould. Toast the bread slices and cut into fingers. Serve with the baked ricotta and the remaining Pesto on the side.

Grill the capsicum until blackened and blistered, then peel off the skin.

Top the capsicum strips with 2 teaspoons of the pesto mixture.

Bake the ricotta cakes until they are firm and golden.

GRILLED FIGS IN PROSCIUTTO

Preparation time: 10 minutes
Cooking time: 15 minutes
Makes 24

50 g unsalted butter
2 tablespoons orange juice
6 small–medium fresh figs
6 long thin slices of prosciutto,
   trimmed of excess fat
24 sage leaves

1 Place the butter in a small heavy-based saucepan. Melt over low heat, then cook the butter for 8–10 minutes, or until the froth subsides and the milk solids appear as brown specks on the bottom of the saucepan. Strain the butter into a clean bowl by pouring it through a strainer lined with a clean tea towel or paper towel. Stir the orange juice into the strained butter.
2 Gently slice the figs lengthways into quarters. Cut each slice of prosciutto into four even strips. Sit a sage leaf on each fig segment, then wrap a piece of prosciutto around the middle of each one, with the ends tucked under the bottom of the fig. Arrange the figs, cut-side-up, on a baking tray and brush lightly with the butter mixture.
3 Move the grill tray to its lowest position, then preheat the grill to hot. Place the baking tray of figs on the grill tray and grill the figs for 1–1½ minutes, or until the prosciutto becomes slightly crispy. Serve hot or at room temperature. If you are serving the figs hot, provide serviettes to avoid burnt fingers.

COOK'S FILE

Note: Because figs are a seasonal fruit, you will need to check their availability with your greengrocer before planning your menu. It is wise to buy a few extra figs than you think you will need because their delicate flesh is easily damaged in transport.
Think ahead: The figs can be wrapped up to 6 hours in advance and covered in plastic wrap. Cook them just before serving.

Variation: You can adapt this recipe to make the popular party food snack, Devils on horseback by using pitted prunes instead of figs. Soak 24 wooden skewers in water for 30 minutes. Wrap a strip of prosciutto around each prune and secure with a skewer. Brush with the butter mixture and cook under a preheated grill for about 1 minute, or until the prosciutto goes crispy. Another favourite is Angels on horseback. It is very similar to Devils on horseback, but uses oysters instead of prunes. Either use 24 oysters on the shell or bottled oysters. Remove the oysters from their shells, or drain from the bottling liquid.

Strain the butter through a strainer lined with a clean tea towel.

Sit a sage leaf on a fig piece, then wrap a piece of prosciutto around the outside.

PARMESAN PEARS

Preparation time: 15 minutes
Total cooking time: 10 minutes
Serves 6

3 firm ripe pears
40 g (1⅓ oz) butter
6 thin slices pancetta, finely chopped
2 spring onions, finely sliced

¾ cup (60 g/2 oz) fresh white breadcrumbs
⅓ cup (35 g/1¼ oz) grated Parmesan

1 Cut the pears in half and remove the cores with a melon baller or teaspoon. Melt the butter in a frying pan. Brush the pears with a little melted butter and place, cut-side-up, on an oven tray. Put under a pre-heated grill for 4 minutes, or until heated through.

2 Add the pancetta and onions to the remaining butter in the pan. Cook until the onions are soft but not brown. Add the breadcrumbs and black pepper to taste.
3 Scatter the pancetta mixture over the pears, sprinkle with Parmesan and grill until golden brown. Serve warm as an entrée, or with roast chicken.

COOK'S FILE
Note: Nashi pears are also suitable.

A melon baller is ideal for cutting out the cores of the pears.

Cook the pancetta and spring onions until soft. Add the breadcrumbs and pepper.

Sprinkle the Parmesan over the pears and grill until golden brown.

MARINATED BOCCONCINI

Preparation time: 15 minutes
+ 3 days refrigeration
Total cooking time: 5 minutes
Serves 8

400 g (13 oz) bocconcini, sliced
150 g (5 oz) jar sun-dried capsicums
   in oil
1 cup (50 g/1¾ oz) small fresh basil
   leaves
1¼ cups (315 ml/10 fl oz) extra virgin
   olive oil
¼ cup (60 ml/2 fl oz) lemon juice

1 Dry the bocconcini with paper
towels. Drain the capsicums,
retaining the oil in a pan, and cut
into strips. Gently crush the basil
leaves. Pour 1 cup (250 ml/8 fl oz)
of the olive oil into the pan with the
reserved oil and gently heat for
5 minutes. Stir the lemon juice into
the warmed oil.
2 Put a layer of bocconcini slices in a
wide-necked 3-cup (750 ml/24 fl oz)
sterilised clip-top jar. Sprinkle with
cracked pepper. Put a thin layer of
basil leaves on top of the cheese and
cover with some of the capsicum.
Continue layering, then cover with
the warmed oil, using the remaining
olive oil if necessary. Seal the jar and
marinate in the refrigerator for 3
days. Return to room temperature
and drain before serving.

COOK'S FILE
Note: To sterilise a storage jar, rinse
with boiling water then place in a
warm oven until completely dry.

*Drain the oil from the capsicums into a
small pan.*

*Gently crush the basil leaves with a
knife to release more of the flavour.*

*Continue layering the bocconcini, basil and
capsicum and cover with the warmed oil.*

GARLIC AND HERB MARINATED ARTICHOKES

Preparation time: 20 minutes
+ overnight refrigeration
Total cooking time: Nil
Serves 8 (as part of an antipasto platter)

2 cloves garlic, chopped
½ cup (125 ml/4 fl oz) olive oil

2 tablespoons finely chopped fresh dill
¼ cup (15 g/½ oz) finely chopped fresh parsley
2 tablespoons finely chopped fresh basil
2 tablespoons lemon juice
2 x 400 g (13 oz) canned artichokes
¼ cup (40 g/1¼ oz) finely diced red capsicum

1 To make the marinade, whisk together the garlic, oil, herbs and lemon juice in a bowl. Season with salt and cracked black pepper.
2 Drain the artichokes and add to the bowl with the capsicum. Mix well to coat. Cover and marinate in the refrigerator overnight. Serve as part of an antipasto platter or use in salads.

COOK'S FILE

Storage time: The artichokes will keep in an airtight container in the refrigerator for up to 1 week.

Use a sharp knife to finely chop the fresh dill.

Combine the garlic, oil, herbs and lemon juice to make the marinade.

Drain the artichokes well before adding to the marinade.

CHICKEN LIVER PATÉ WITH PISTACHIO NUTS AND PROSCIUTTO

Preparation time: 20 minutes
+ 3 hours refrigeration
Total cooking time: 15 minutes
Serves 10

6 very thin slices prosciutto
2 tablespoons butter
3 tablespoons olive oil
80 g (2¾ oz) finely diced bacon
1 onion, finely chopped
2 cloves garlic, crushed
500 g (1 lb) chicken livers
3 bay leaves
⅓ cup (80 ml/2¾ fl oz) sherry or
   brandy
125 g (4 oz) butter, softened
⅓ cup (50 g/1¾ oz) pistachio nuts,
   toasted

1 Line a 1.5 litre loaf tin with foil. Then line with the prosciutto so that it hangs over the sides, making sure each slice overlaps. Heat the butter and oil and cook the bacon, onion and garlic for 5–6 minutes, or until the onion is softened but not browned.
2 Trim the chicken livers of any fat and veins. Add them to the pan with the bay leaves. Increase the heat to hot and cook for 3–4 minutes, or until the livers are brown on the outside, but still pink on the inside.
3 Add the sherry and simmer, stirring continuously, for 3 minutes, or until the liquid has almost disappeared. Remove the bay leaves. Put the mixture in a food processor and blend to a very fine texture. Gradually add the butter and blend until smooth. Season, then stir in the pistachios.
4 Spoon the paté mixture into the tin and fold the prosciutto over the top to enclose it. Refrigerate for at least 3 hours before serving. Cut into slices to serve.

COOK'S FILE

Note: The flavour, colour and texture of the pâté will improve after 2 days, and it will also become easier to slice. Keep refrigerated for 3–4 days.

Line the tin with the prosciutto with each slice overlapping.

Remove the fat and veins from the chicken livers before cooking.

Add the sherry and simmer until most of the liquid has disappeared.

Stir the toasted pistachio nuts through the liver mixture.

SEMI-DRIED TOMATOES

Preparation time:
10 minutes
+ 24 hours refrigeration
Total cooking time: 2 hours
30 minutes
Fills a 500 ml (16 fl oz) jar

16 Roma tomatoes

3 tablespoons fresh thyme,
  chopped
2 tablespoons olive oil

1 Preheat the oven to warm 160°C (315°F/Gas 2–3). Cut the tomatoes into quarters lengthways and lay them skin-side-down on a wire rack in a baking tray.
2 Sprinkle with 1 teaspoon of salt, 1 teaspoon of cracked black pepper and the thyme and cook in the oven

for 2½ hours. Check occasionally to make sure the tomatoes don't burn.
3 Toss the tomatoes in the olive oil and leave to cool before packing into sterilised jars and sealing. Store in the refrigerator for 24 hours before using. Eaten within 3–4 days.

COOK'S FILE
Note: To sterilise a storage jar, rinse in boiling water then place in a warm oven until dry. Do not dry with a tea towel.

Cut the tomatoes into quarters and lay them skin-side-down on a wire rack.

Season the tomatoes with salt, cracked pepper and fresh thyme.

Cover the tomatoes with olive oil and toss until well coated.

ASPARAGUS AND PROSCIUTTO BUNDLES WITH HOLLANDAISE

Preparation time: 10 minutes
Cooking time: 15 minutes
Makes 24

24 spears fresh asparagus, trimmed
8 slices prosciutto, cut into thirds lengthways

HOLLANDAISE
175 g butter
4 egg yolks
1 tablespoon lemon juice
ground white pepper

1 Blanch the asparagus in boiling salted water for 2 minutes, then drain and refresh in cold water. Pat dry, then cut the spears in half. Lay the bottom half of each spear next to its tip, then secure together by wrapping a piece of prosciutto around them.
2 To make the Hollandaise: Melt the butter in a small saucepan. Skim any froth off the top. Cool the butter a little. Combine the egg yolks and 2 tablespoons of water in a small heatproof bowl placed over a saucepan of simmering water, making sure the base of the bowl does not touch the water. Using a wire whisk, beat for about 3–4 minutes, or until the mixture is thick and foamy. Make sure the bowl does not get too hot or you will end up with scrambled eggs. Add the butter

slowly, a little at a time at first, whisking well between each addition. Keep adding the butter in a thin stream, whisking continuously, until all the butter has been used. Try to avoid using the milky whey in the bottom of the pan, but don't worry if a little gets in. Stir in the lemon juice and season with salt and white pepper. Place in a bowl and serve warm with the asparagus.

COOK'S FILE

Hollandaise can be made 1 day in advance and stored, covered, in the fridge. To reheat, put the bowl over a saucepan of simmering water, making sure it does not touch the water, and whisk until just warm.

Briefly cook the asparagus in boiling water, then drain.

Wrap the tip and bottom end of each spear in a piece of prosciutto.

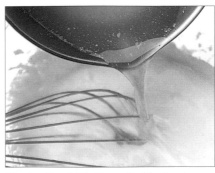

Gradually whisk the melted butter into the hollandaise mixture.

MARINATING OLIVES

Cracking the olives means to cut a slit around the olives using a sharp knife to allow flavours to infuse into the olives. To sterilise the storage jar, rinse with boiling water then place in a warm oven to dry. Olive oil solidifies with refrigeration, so take the olives out of the fridge 30 minutes before serving.

MIXED OLIVES WITH HERBS

Place 200 g small black olives (Riverina or Ligurian), 200 g cracked green olives, 200 g cracked Kalamata olives, 1 tablespoon fresh oregano leaves, 3 sprigs fresh thyme, 2 bay leaves, 1 teaspoon paprika and 2 teaspoons lemon zest in a bowl and toss well. Spoon into a 1 litre sterilised wide-necked jar and add 450 ml olive oil. Marinate for 1–2 weeks in the fridge. Will keep for 1 month in the fridge.

CHILLI OLIVES

Soak 3 thinly sliced garlic cloves in vinegar or lemon juice for 24 hours. Drain and mix in a bowl with 500 g cured (wrinkled) black olives, 3 tablespoons chopped fresh flat-leaf parsley, 1 tablespoon dried chilli flakes, 3 teaspoons crushed coriander seeds and 2 teaspoons crushed cumin seeds. Spoon into a 1 litre sterilised wide-necked jar and add 500 ml olive oil. Marinate for 1–2 weeks in the fridge. Keeps for 1 month in the fridge.

ANCHOVY-STUFFED GREEN OLIVES WITH PRESERVED LEMON

Toss 500 g anchovy-stuffed green olives in a bowl with ½ preserved lemon, pith and flesh removed, rind washed and thinly sliced, 2 tablespoons of liquid from the lemons and 1 tablespoon coriander seeds. Spoon into a 1 litre sterilised wide-necked jar and add 500 ml olive oil. Marinate for 1–2 weeks in the fridge. Will keep for 1 month in the fridge.

LEMON, THYME AND ROSEMARY OLIVES

Soak 2 thinly sliced garlic cloves in vinegar or lemon juice for 24 hours. Drain and place in a bowl with 500 g cracked Kalamata olives, 2 crushed bay leaves, 4 slices lemon, cut into quarters, 3 sprigs fresh thyme, 1 sprig of fresh rosemary, ½ teaspoon black peppercorns and ¼ cup (60 ml) lemon juice, and toss to combine. Spoon into a 1 litre sterilised wide-necked jar and pour in 500 ml olive oil. Marinate for 1–2 weeks in the fridge. Will keep for 1 month in the fridge.

CORIANDER AND ORANGE OLIVES

Place 500 g jumbo green olives in a large bowl and add 2 teaspoons crushed coriander seeds, 3 teaspoons orange zest, ¼ cup (60 ml) orange juice, ¼ teaspoon cayenne pepper, 3 tablespoons chopped fresh coriander leaves and toss to combine thoroughly. Carefully spoon into a 1 litre, sterilised wide-necked jar and pour in 500 ml olive oil or enough to completely cover. Leave to marinate for 1–2 weeks in the fridge. Will keep for 1 month in the fridge.

FENNEL, ORANGE AND DILL OLIVES

Soak 2 thinly sliced garlic cloves in vinegar or lemon juice for 24 hours. Drain and place the garlic in a large bowl with 500 g cracked black olives, 4 thin slices orange cut into quarters, 2 teaspoons crushed fennel seeds and 2 tablespoons chopped fresh dill and toss to combine well. Spoon into a 1 litre sterilised wide necked jar and pour in 500 ml olive oil or enough to completely cover. Marinate for 1–2 weeks in the fridge. Will keep for 1 month in the fridge.

Left to right: Mixed Olives with Herbs; Chilli Olives; Anchovy-stuffed Green Olives with Preserved Lemon; Lemon, Thyme and Rosemary Olives; Coriander and Orange Olives; Fennel, Orange and Dill Olives.

SOUPS

SEAFOOD SOUP

Preparation time: 40 minutes
Total cooking time: 1 hour 20 minutes
Serves 4–6

4–6 tomatoes
500 g (1 lb) raw king prawns
1 raw lobster tail
1–2 fish heads
1 cup (250 ml/8 fl oz) red wine
3 onions, finely chopped
6 cloves garlic, crushed
3 bay leaves
¼ cup (60 ml/2 fl oz) olive oil
1 leek, finely sliced
¼ cup (60 g/2 oz) tomato paste
small piece of orange rind
500 g (1 lb) white fish fillet,
    cut into small pieces
12 mussels, firmly closed, scrubbed
    and beards removed
200 g (6½ oz) scallops with corals
½ cup (30 g/1 oz) chopped parsley
¼ cup (15 g/½ oz) shredded basil
    leaves

1 Score a cross in the base of each tomato. Cover with boiling water for 1 minute, plunge in cold water, drain and peel away the skins.

2 To make the fish stock, peel and devein the prawns and set the shells, heads and tails aside. Shell the lobster tail, keeping the shell and chopping the meat. Put the lobster shell, fish heads, prawn shells, heads and tails in a large pan. Add the wine, 1 onion, 2 cloves garlic, 1 bay leaf and 2 cups (500 ml/16 fl oz) of water. Bring to the boil, reduce the heat and simmer for 20 minutes. Strain through a fine sieve, reserving the stock.

3 Heat the oil in a large, heavy-based pan. Add the leek and remaining onion and garlic. Cover and simmer, stirring occasionally, over low heat for 20 minutes, or until browned. Add the tomato, remaining bay leaves, tomato paste and orange rind and stir well. Remove the lid and continue to cook for 10 minutes, stirring occasionally. Add the reserved fish stock, bring to the boil, reduce the heat and simmer for 10 minutes, stirring occasionally.

4 Add the prawns, lobster, fish pieces, mussels and scallops. Simmer, covered, for 4–5 minutes. Discard any unopened mussels, the rind and bay leaves. Add the herbs and season to taste with salt and freshly ground black pepper.

Cut on either side of the soft underside of the lobster tail, and lift up.

Strain through a fine sieve, reserving the stock.

MINESTRONE WITH PESTO

Preparation time: 25 minutes
+ overnight soaking
Total cooking time: 2 hours
Serves 6

125 g dried borlotti beans
1 large onion, coarsely chopped
2 cloves garlic
3 tablespoons coarsely chopped
   fresh flat-leaf parsley
60 g pancetta, chopped
3 tablespoons olive oil
1 celery stick, halved lengthways,
   then cut into 1 cm slices
1 carrot, halved lengthways, then
   cut into 1 cm slices
1 potato, diced
2 teaspoons tomato paste
400 g can Italian diced tomatoes
6 fresh basil leaves, roughly torn
2 litres chicken or vegetable stock
2 thin zucchini, cut into 1.5 cm slices
¾ cup (115 g) shelled peas
60 g green beans, cut into
   4 cm lengths
80 g silverbeet leaves, shredded
75 g ditalini or other small pasta

PESTO
1 cup (30 g) loosely packed fresh
   basil leaves
20 g lightly toasted pine nuts
2 cloves garlic
100 ml olive oil
¼ cup (25 g) freshly grated Parmesan

1 Put the beans in a large bowl,
cover with water and soak overnight.
Drain and rinse under cold water.
2 Place the onion, garlic, parsley
and pancetta in a food processor and

process until fine. Heat the oil in a
large saucepan, add the pancetta
mixture and cook over a low heat,
stirring occasionally, for about
8–10 minutes.
3 Add the celery, carrot and potato,
and cook for 5 minutes, then stir in
the tomato paste, tomato, basil and
borlotti beans. Season with freshly
ground black pepper. Add the stock
and bring slowly to the boil. Cover
and simmer, stirring occasionally, for
1 hour 30 minutes.
4 Season and add the zucchini, peas,
green beans, silverbeet and pasta.

Simmer for 8–10 minutes, or until
the vegetables and pasta are al dente.
5 To make the Pesto: Ccombine the
basil, pine nuts and garlic with a
pinch of salt in a food processor.
Process until finely chopped. With
the motor running, slowly add the
olive oil. Transfer to a bowl and stir
in the Parmesan and freshly ground
black pepper to taste. Serve the soup
in bowls with the Pesto on top.

*Cook the processed onion, garlic, parsley
and pancetta mixture.*

*Simmer until the pasta and vegetables
are al dente.*

*Stir the Parmesan into the finely chopped
basil mixture.*

PAPPA AL POMADORO
(Tomato bread soup)

Preparation time: 20 minutes
+ 5 minutes standing
Total cooking time: 25 minutes
Serves 4

750 g vine-ripened tomatoes
1 loaf (450 g) day-old crusty Italian
 bread
1 tablespoon olive oil
3 cloves garlic, crushed
1 tablespoon tomato paste
1.25 litres hot vegetable stock
4 tablespoons torn fresh basil leaves
2–3 tablespoons extra virgin
 olive oil
extra virgin olive oil, extra, to serve

1 Score a cross in the base of each tomato. Place in a bowl of boiling water for 1 minute, then plunge into cold water and peel the skin away from the cross. Cut the tomatoes in half and scoop out the seeds with a teaspoon. Chop the tomato flesh.
2 Remove most of the crust from the bread and discard. Cut the bread into 3 cm pieces.
3 Heat the oil in a large saucepan. Add the garlic, tomato and tomato paste, then reduce the heat and simmer, stirring occasionally, for 10–15 minutes, or until reduced and thickened. Add the stock and bring to the boil, stirring for 2–3 minutes. Reduce the heat to medium, add the bread pieces and cook, stirring, for 5 minutes, or until the bread softens and absorbs most of the liquid. Add more stock or water if necessary.
4 Stir in the torn basil leaves and extra virgin olive oil, and leave for

5 minutes so the flavours have time to develop. Drizzle with a little extra virgin olive oil.

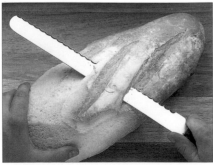

Remove most of the crust from the loaf of bread and discard.

Reduce the heat and simmer for 15 minutes, or until reduced.

Add the bread pieces to the tomato mixture and cook, stirring.

MINESTRONE PRIMAVERA

Preparation time: 15 minutes
Total cooking time: 40 minutes
Serves 4–6

¼ cup (60 ml/2 fl oz) olive oil
45 g (1½ oz) pancetta, finely chopped
2 onions, chopped
2 cloves garlic, thinly sliced
2 small sticks celery, sliced
8 cups (2 litres) chicken stock
⅓ cup (50 g/1¾ oz) macaroni
2 zucchini, chopped

2 cups (150 g/5 oz) shredded savoy cabbage
1½ cups (185 g/6 oz) green beans, chopped
1 cup (155 g/5 oz) frozen peas
1 cup (40 g/1¼ oz) shredded English spinach leaves
¼ cup (15 g/½ oz) chopped basil
grated Parmesan, to serve

1 Put the oil, pancetta, onion, garlic and celery in a large pan and stir occasionally over low heat for 8 minutes, or until the vegetables are soft but not brown. Add the stock and bring to the boil. Simmer, covered, for 10 minutes.

2 Add the macaroni and boil for 12 minutes, or until almost tender. Stir in the zucchini, cabbage, beans and peas and simmer for 5 minutes. Add the spinach and basil and simmer for 2 minutes. Season to taste and serve with the grated Parmesan.

COOK'S FILE
Serving suggestion: Serve with the Zucchini and olive bread on page 195.

Using a sharp knife, cut the pancetta into strips then chop finely.

Chop the zucchini and finely shred the savoy cabbage.

Add the shredded spinach and basil to the soup.

PASTA AND BEAN SOUP

Preparation time: 15 minutes
+ overnight soaking
+ 10 minutes resting
Total cooking time:
1 hour 45 minutes
Serves 4

200 g dried borlotti beans
¼ cup (60 ml) olive oil
90 g piece pancetta, finely diced
1 onion, finely chopped
2 cloves garlic, crushed
1 celery stick, thinly sliced
1 carrot, diced
1 bay leaf
1 sprig fresh rosemary
1 sprig fresh flat-leaf parsley
400 g can diced tomatoes, drained
1.6 litres vegetable stock
2 tablespoons finely chopped fresh
    flat-leaf parsley
150 g ditalini or other small dried
    pasta
extra virgin olive oil, to drizzle
freshly grated Parmesan,
    to serve

1 Place the beans in a large bowl, cover with cold water and leave to soak overnight. Drain away the water and rinse the beans well.
2 Heat the oil in a large saucepan, add the pancetta, onion, garlic, celery and carrot, and cook over medium heat for 5 minutes, or until golden. Season with pepper. Add the bay leaf, rosemary, parsley, tomato, stock and beans, and bring to the boil. Reduce the heat and simmer for 1½ hours, or until the beans are tender. Add more boiling water if necessary to maintain the liquid level.

3 Discard the bay leaf, rosemary and parsley sprigs. Scoop out 1 cup of the bean mixture and purée in a food processor or blender. Return to the pan, season with salt and ground black pepper, and add the parsley and pasta. Simmer for 6 minutes, or until the pasta is al dente. Remove from the heat and set aside for 10 minutes.

Serve drizzled with extra virgin olive oil and garnished with Parmesan.

COOK'S FILE
Note: If you prefer, you can use three 400 g cans drained borlotti beans. Simmer with the other vegetables for 30 minutes.

Cook the pancetta, onion, garlic, celery and carrot for 5 minutes.

Purée 1 cup of the bean mixture in a food processor.

Add the pasta to the soup and cook until al dente.

PUMPKIN AND RED LENTIL SOUP

Preparation time: 15 minutes
Total cooking time: 30 minutes
Serves 4

1 tablespoon olive oil
1 long red chilli, seeded
   and chopped
1 onion, finely chopped
500 g butternut pumpkin, chopped
350 g orange sweet potato, chopped
1 litre vegetable stock
½ cup (125 g) red lentils
1 tablespoon tahini

1 Heat the oil in a large saucepan over medium heat, add the chilli and onion and cook for 2–3 minutes, or until the onion is soft. Reduce the heat to low, add the pumpkin and sweet potato and cook, covered, for 8 minutes, stirring occasionally.
2 Increase the heat to high, add the stock and bring to the boil. Reduce the heat to low, and simmer, covered, for 10 minutes. Add the lentils and cook, covered, for 7 minutes, or until they are tender.

3 Transfer the mixture to a blender or food processor, add the tahini and blend until smooth. Return to the saucepan and gently heat until warmed through. Garnish with chilli and serve with crusty bread.

COOK'S FILE
Note: The soup can be made up to a day ahead. Keep covered with plastic wrap in the refrigerator and reheat in a saucepan or in the microwave.

Wearing rubber gloves, remove the seeds and membranes from the chilli and chop.

Stir the pumpkin and sweet potato into the onion mixture.

Blend the soup and tahini in a food processor until smooth.

BROCCOLI AND PINE NUT SOUP

Preparation time: 10 minutes
Total cooking time: 30 minutes
Serves 6

30 g (1 oz) butter
1 onion, finely chopped
6 cups (1.5 litres) chicken stock

750 g (1½ lb) fresh broccoli
⅓ cup (50 g/1⅔ oz) pine nuts
extra pine nuts, to serve

1 Melt the butter in a large pan and cook the onion until soft but not browned. Add the stock and bring to the boil.
2 Remove the florets from the broccoli and set aside. Chop the broccoli stalks and add to pan. Reduce heat, cover and simmer for 15 minutes.

Add the florets and simmer, uncovered, for 10 minutes, or until tender. Allow to cool completely.
3 Add the pine nuts and blend until smooth in a food processor (you may need to blend in batches, depending on the size of your processor). Season to taste with salt and pepper, then gently reheat. Sprinkle with extra pine nuts to serve. Delicious with toasted foccacia, drizzled with extra virgin olive oil.

Cook the onion until soft and then add the chicken stock.

Remove the florets from the broccoli and chop the stalks into even-sized pieces.

Let the soup cool, to prevent burns, then process with the pine nuts.

OSSO BUCO, BARLEY AND VEGETABLE SOUP

Preparation time: 25 minutes
Total cooking time: 50 minutes
Serves 6

500 g (1 lb) veal shanks with bones
   (osso buco), cut into
   5 cm (2 inch) pieces
   (ask your butcher to do this)
2 tablespoons olive oil
1 onion, diced
1–2 garlic cloves, crushed
425 g (14 oz) can chopped tomatoes
1 tablespoon tomato paste
½ teaspoon dried oregano
6 cups (1.5 litres) beef stock
300 g (10 oz) potatoes, cubed
300 g (10 oz) pumpkin, cubed
¾ cup (165 g/5½ oz) pearl barley
200 g (6½ oz) zucchini, sliced

1 Trim the meat from the bones and cut into cubes. Scrape out the marrow from the bones, if you want to use it, and discard the bones. Heat the oil in a heavy-based pan and brown the meat and marrow, in batches if necessary, until rich brown. Remove and drain on paper towels. Set the fried marrow aside, to garnish.
2 Add the onion to the pan and cook for 4–5 minutes over low heat; then add the garlic and cook for 1 minute longer. Add the meat, tomato, tomato paste, oregano, stock, potato and pumpkin.
3 Wash the barley in a sieve until the water runs clean, then drain and add to the soup. Bring to the boil, reduce the heat to low and simmer, covered, for 20 minutes. Add the zucchini and cook, covered, for 10 minutes, or until the barley is cooked. Serve garnished with the fried marrow.

COOK'S FILE

Note: Osso buco (or ossobuco) is the Italian for marrowbone. It is a stew made with the knuckle of veal, usually served in a tomato sauce.

Trim the meat from the bones and cut into cubes.

Add the meat, tomato, tomato paste, oregano, stock, potato and pumpkin.

Wash the barley in a sieve under running water until the water runs clear.

Add the zucchini to the boiling soup and cook for 10 minutes.

ROASTED VEGETABLE SOUP

Preparation time: 30 minutes
Total cooking time: 1 hour 35 minutes
Serves 6

2 carrots, cut into large pieces
1 parsnip, cut into large pieces
500 g (1 lb) unpeeled pumpkin, cut into large pieces
350 g (11 oz) unpeeled sweet potato, cut into large pieces

1 red capsicum, cut into large pieces
2 onions, halved
4 cloves garlic, unpeeled
3 cups (750 ml/24 fl oz) vegetable stock
sour cream and thyme, to serve

1 Preheat the oven to moderate 180°C (350°F/Gas 4). Put the vegetables in a large greased baking dish and brush lightly with some olive oil.
2 Bake for 1 hour, turning often. Remove the capsicum. Bake for 30 minutes longer; cool the vegetables slightly. Remove the skin from the capsicum; place in a food processor with the carrot, parsnip and onion.
3 Scrape the pumpkin and sweet potato flesh into the processor and squeeze in the garlic pulp. Add half the stock and purée until smooth. Place in a pan with the remaining stock and heat through. Season and serve with sour cream and thyme.

COOK'S FILE
Serving suggestion: Serve with Rosemary bread trios on page 189.

Cut the carrots, parsnip, pumpkin and sweet potato into large pieces.

Using your fingers, carefully peel away the blackened capsicum skin.

Using a teaspoon, scrape the flesh from the sweet potato and pumpkin.

LEMON-SCENTED BROTH WITH TORTELLINI

Preparation time: 10 minutes
Total cooking time: 18 minutes
Serves 4–6

1 lemon
½ cup good quality white wine
440 g can chicken consommé
3 cups water
⅓ cup chopped fresh parsley
black pepper, to taste
375 g fresh or dried veal- or
   chicken-filled tortellini
2 tablespoons grated Parmesan

1 Using a vegetable peeler, peel wide strips from lemon. Remove white pith with a small sharp knife and cut 3 of the wide pieces into fine strips; set aside the fine strips for garnish.
2 Place wide lemon strips, white wine, consomme and water in a large deep pan. Cook for 10 minutes over low heat. Remove lemon rind from pan and bring mixture to the boil.
3 Add 2 tablespoons of parsley, pepper and tortellini to pan. Cook for 6–7 minutes or until pasta is just tender. Garnish with remaining parsley and fine strips of lemon.
4 Grate some fresh Parmesan cheese and sprinkle over the top.

COOK'S FILE
Storage time: If desired, the day before broth is required, follow recipe to the removal of lemon rind from pan. Just before serving, bring mixture to the boil; add chopped parsley, black pepper and tortellini. Continue with recipe.
Variations: Use chopped basil instead of parsley or different types of tortellini.

BACON AND PEA SOUP

Preparation time: 20 minutes
Total cooking time: 15 minutes
Serves 4–6

1 large onion
4 rashers bacon
50 g butter
1 stick celery, chopped into small
    pieces

2 litres chicken stock
1 cup frozen green peas
250 g risoni
2 tablespoons chopped fresh parsley
pepper, to taste

1 Peel onion and chop finely.
Trim rind and excess fat from bacon;
chop bacon into small pieces.
2 Place bacon, butter, onion and
celery in large heavy-based pan.
Cook for 5 minutes over low heat,
stirring occasionally. Add chicken

stock and peas; simmer, covered,
5 minutes. Increase heat and add
pasta; cook, uncovered, stirring
occasionally, for 5 minutes.
3 Add chopped parsley and pepper
just before serving.

COOK'S FILE
Storage time: You can make this soup
the day before required and store in an
airtight container in refrigerator. Gently
reheat before serving.

CREAM OF ASPARAGUS SOUP

Preparation time: 20 minutes
Total cooking time: 55 minutes
Serves 4–6

1 kg (2 lb) asparagus spears
30 g (1 oz) butter
1 onion, finely chopped
1 litre (4 cups) chicken stock
¼ cup (7 g/¼ oz) basil leaves,
   chopped
1 teaspoon celery salt
1 cup (250 ml/8 fl oz) cream

1 Break off the woody ends from the asparagus and trim off the tips. Blanch the tips in boiling water for 1–2 minutes, refresh in cold water and set aside. Chop the remaining asparagus spears into large pieces.
2 Melt the butter in a large pan and cook the onion for 3–4 minutes over medium-low heat, or until soft and golden. Add the asparagus spears and cook for 1–2 minutes, stirring continuously.
3 Add the chicken stock, basil and celery salt. Bring to the boil, reduce the heat and simmer gently, covered, for 30 minutes.
4 Check that the asparagus is well cooked and soft. If not, simmer for a further 10 minutes. Set aside and allow to cool slightly.
5 Pour into a processor and process in batches until smooth. Then sieve into a clean pan. Return to the heat, pour in the cream and gently reheat. Do not allow the soup to boil. Season to taste with salt and white pepper.
6 Serve immediately, placing the asparagus tips on top of the soup.

COOK'S FILE
Hint: If you are not using home-made stock, always taste before adding seasoning to your soup—shop-bought stock can be very salty.

Break off the woody ends from the asparagus spears.

Test whether the asparagus is well cooked by piercing it with a fork.

POTATO AND GARLIC SOUP

Preparation time: 15 minutes
Total cooking time: 1 hour 5 minutes
Serves 6

2 bulbs garlic
500 g (1 lb) potatoes
1 onion, finely chopped
2 onions, halved
8 cups (2 litres chicken stock)
chopped chives, to serve

1 Separate the garlic bulbs into cloves and gently crush with the flat side of a knife to split the skin. Peel the cloves and cut in half. Chop the potatoes into small cubes.
2 Heat the olive oil in a large frying pan, add the onion and garlic and cook over a medium-low heat for 5–10 minutes, or until the garlic is lightly golden. Add the potato and cook over a low heat for 5 minutes. Add the chicken stock and simmer for 40–45 minutes, or until the garlic is very soft and the stock has reduced. Set aside to cool slightly.
3 Process the soup in batches in a food processor until smooth. Return to the pan and add ½ teaspoon of salt, to taste, before adding any more

seasoning. Reheat gently before serving. Serve with sprinkling of chopped chives.

COOK'S FILE
Note: If you don't have time to make stock, try the carton stocks from supermarkets, which contain less salt and additives than cubes. If you are not using home-made stock, make sure you taste the soup before seasoning as some shop-bought stocks are very salty. Season after cooking as long simmering tends to concentrate the flavours of the soup.

Two bulbs may seem a lot, but once it is cooked garlic takes on a mellow flavour.

Crush each clove with the flat side of a knife to split the skin.

Simmer the stock until the garlic cloves are very soft.

PASTA AND GNOCCHI

SPAGHETTI PUTTANESCA

Preparation time: 15 minutes
Total cooking time: 20 minutes
Serves 4–6

500 g spaghetti or fettuccine
2 tablespoons olive oil
3 cloves garlic, crushed
2 tablespoons chopped fresh parsley
¼–½ teaspoon chilli flakes or powder
2 x 425 g can tomatoes
1 tablespoon capers
3 anchovy fillets, chopped
¼ cup black olives
black pepper, to taste

1 Add spaghetti or fettuccine to a large pan of rapidly boiling water. Cook pasta until just tender and drain immediately. Return drained pasta to pan.
2 While pasta is cooking, heat oil in a heavy-based frying pan. Add garlic, parsley and chilli flakes and cook, stirring, 1 minute over medium heat.
3 Add undrained, crushed tomatoes and stir to combine. Reduce heat and simmer, covered, for 5 minutes.
4 Add capers, anchovies and olives and cook, stirring, for 5 minutes. Add black pepper; stir. Add sauce to pasta and toss gently until evenly distributed. Serve immediately in warmed pasta bowls.

COOK'S FILE
Hint: Leave tomatoes in the can and chop with a pair of kitchen scissors.

BUCATINI WITH FARMHOUSE SAUCE

Preparation time: 20 minutes
Total cooking time: 25 minutes
Serves 4–6

2 tablespoons olive oil
250 g mushrooms
1 medium eggplant
2 cloves garlic, crushed
825 g can tomatoes

500 g bucatini or spaghetti
salt and pepper, to taste
¼ cup chopped fresh parsley

1 Heat oil in a medium heavy-based pan. Wipe mushrooms with paper towels; slice. Chop eggplant into small cubes.
2 Add mushrooms, eggplant and garlic to pan and cook, stirring, for 4 minutes. Add undrained, crushed tomatoes; cover and simmer for 15 minutes. While sauce is cooking, add pasta to a large pan of rapidly boiling

water and cook until just tender. Drain and return to pan.
3 Season the sauce with salt and pepper. Add chopped parsley to pan and stir. Add sauce to the pasta and toss well. Serve immediately in warmed pasta bowls.

COOK'S FILE
Hint: If the pasta is cooked before you are ready to serve you can prevent it sticking together by adding a little olive oil after draining it. Toss oil through the pasta.

PASTA AND SPINACH TIMBALE

Preparation time: 15 minutes
Total cooking time: 35 minutes
Serves 6

30 g butter or margarine
1 tablespoon olive oil
1 onion, chopped
1 bunch cooked, well-drained spinach
8 eggs, beaten
1 cup (250 ml) thickened or pouring
    cream
100 g spaghetti or tagliolini, cooked
½ cup grated Cheddar cheese

½ cup freshly grated Parmesan
    cheese
salt and freshly ground black pepper,
    to taste

1 Preheat oven to moderate 180°C. Brush six 1-cup capacity moulds with melted butter or oil. Line bases with baking paper. Heat butter and oil together in a frying pan. Add onion and stir over low heat until onion is tender. Add well-drained spinach and cook for 1 minute. Remove from heat and allow to cool. Whisk in eggs and cream. Stir in the spaghetti or tagliolini, grated cheeses, salt and pepper; stir well. Spoon into prepared moulds.

2 Place moulds in a baking dish. Pour boiling water into baking dish to come halfway up sides of moulds. Bake for 30–35 minutes or until set. Halfway through cooking, you may need to cover top with a sheet of foil to prevent excess browning. Near the end of cooking time, test timbales with the point of a knife. When cooked, the knife should come out clean.
3 Allow timbales to rest 15 minutes. Run point of a knife around edge of each mould. Invert onto plates.

COOK'S FILE
Hints: Serve with a tomato sauce.

CREAMY PRAWNS WITH FETTUCCINE

Preparation time: 20 minutes
Total cooking time: 15 minutes
Serves 4

500 g fettuccine
500 g green prawns
30 g butter or margarine
1 tablespoon olive oil
6 spring onions, chopped
1 clove garlic, crushed
1 cup (250 ml) thickened or pouring
    cream
salt and freshly ground black pepper,
    to taste
2 tablespoons chopped fresh parsley,
    for serving

1 Add fettuccine to a large pan of rapidly boiling water and cook until just tender. Drain well; return to pan. While fettuccine is cooking, peel and devein prawns.
2 Heat butter and oil in a frying pan. Add spring onion and garlic and stir over low heat 1 minute. Add prawns. Cook for 2–3 minutes or until flesh changes colour. Remove prawns from pan and set aside. Add cream to pan and bring to the boil. Reduce heat and simmer until sauce begins to thicken. Return prawns to pan and add salt and pepper. Simmer for 1 minute.
3 Add prawns and sauce to fettuccine and toss. Serve in warmed pasta bowls. Sprinkle with parsley.

COOK'S FILE
Variations: In step 1, add 1 red capsicum, seeded and sliced, and 1 leek, dark green section removed and white part cleaned thoroughly and sliced very finely. Use scallops instead of prawns or a mixture of both.

PASTITSIO

Preparation time: 20 minutes
Total cooking time: 1 hour
Serves 4–6

250 g tubular spaghetti
250 g tub ricotta cheese
60 g prosciutto, chopped
1 egg, beaten
1 tablespoon freshly grated parmesan
    cheese
¼ teaspoon ground nutmeg
salt and freshly ground black pepper,
    to taste

MEAT SAUCE
2 tablespoons olive oil
1 onion, chopped
1 clove garlic, crushed
500 g beef mince
425 g can tomatoes
½ cup red wine
½ cup beef stock
2 tablespoons tomato
    paste
2 tablespoons chopped fresh parsley
½ teaspoon ground oregano
salt and freshly ground black pepper,
    to taste

CHEESE SAUCE
60 g butter or margarine
¼ cup plain flour
1½ cups milk
1 cup (250 ml) thickened or pouring
    cream
2 eggs, beaten
1 cup freshly grated Cheddar cheese
1/4 teaspoon ground nutmeg
salt and freshly ground black pepper,
    to taste
¼ cup fresh breadcrumbs
¼ cup freshly grated Parmesan
    cheese

1 Preheat oven to moderate 180°C.
Oil a 28 x 20 cm ovenproof dish.
Cook pasta in large pan of rapidly
boiling water until just tender; drain
well. Allow to cool slightly; return to
pan. Add ricotta, prosciutto, egg,
Parmesan, nutmeg, salt and pepper
to pasta. Press into prepared dish.
Set aside.
2 To make Meat Sauce: Heat oil in
large pan. Add onion and garlic; stir
over low heat until onion is tender.
Add mince; brown well, breaking up
with a fork as it cooks. Add
undrained, crushed tomatoes, wine,
stock, tomato paste, parsley, oregano,
salt and pepper; stir. Bring to the

boil. Reduce heat. Simmer,
uncovered, for 20 minutes. Spoon
over the pasta layer. Set aside.
3 To make Cheese Sauce: Melt
butter in medium pan. Add flour
and cook, stirring, for 1 minute.
Remove from heat. Gradually add
milk and cream, stirring until
smooth. Return to heat. Cook,
stirring constantly, until sauce boils
and thickens. Reduce heat; simmer
for 3 minutes. Remove from heat.
Whisk in eggs, cheese, nutmeg, salt
and pepper. Spoon over the meat
layer. Sprinkle with combined
breadcrumbs and Parmesan. Bake
20–25 minutes.

BAKED CANNELLONI MILANESE

Preparation time: 20 minutes
Total cooking time: 1 hour
50 minutes
Serves 4

500 g pork and veal mince
½ cup dry breadcrumbs
½ cup freshly grated Parmesan
    cheese
2 eggs, beaten
1 teaspoon dried oregano
salt and freshly ground black pepper,
    to taste
12–15 cannelloni tubes
375 g fresh ricotta cheese
½ cup freshly grated Parmesan
    cheese, extra
½ cup freshly grated Cheddar cheese

TOMATO SAUCE
425 ml can tomato purée
425 g can tomatoes
2 cloves garlic, crushed
¼ cup chopped fresh basil
freshly ground black pepper,
    to taste

1 Preheat oven to moderate 180°C.
Lightly grease a rectangular casserole
dish. In a medium bowl, combine
mince, breadcrumbs, Parmesan
cheese, beaten egg, oregano and
seasonings. Use a teaspoon to stuff
the cannelloni tubes with mince
mixture. Set aside.
2 To make Tomato Sauce: Place
tomato purée, undrained, crushed
tomatoes and garlic in medium pan.
Bring to the boil. Reduce heat.
Simmer for 15 minutes. Add basil
and pepper and stir well.
3 Spoon half the Tomato Sauce
over the base of prepared dish.
4 Arrange the stuffed cannelloni
tubes on top. Cover with remaining
sauce. Spread with ricotta cheese.
Sprinkle with combined Parmesan
and Cheddar cheeses. Bake, covered
with foil, for 1 hour. Uncover and
bake for another 15 minutes or until
golden. Cut into squares for serving.

COOK'S FILE
Hint: Serve with tomato quarters and a
green salad. Garnish with fresh herbs.

PASTA WITH CLAMS

Preparation time: 25 minutes
Total cooking time: 20 minutes
Serves 4

500 g small shell pasta
1 kg clams
1 tablespoon olive oil
2 cloves garlic, crushed
2 x 425 g cans tomatoes
¼ cup red wine
2 tablespoons chopped fresh parsley
1 teaspoon sugar
salt and freshly ground black pepper,
    to taste

1 Heat a large pan of water until water is boiling rapidly. Add pasta and cook until just tender. Drain and keep warm. Blend 2 tablespoons each of salt and plain flour with enough water to make a paste. Add to a large pan of cold water and soak shellfish in mixture overnight. This will draw out sand from inside shells. Scrub shells well. Rinse and drain.
2 Heat oil in a large pan. Add garlic and cook over low heat for 30 seconds. Add undrained, crushed tomatoes, wine, parsley, sugar, salt and pepper; stir. Bring to the boil. Reduce heat and simmer, stirring occasionally, for 5 minutes.
3 Add scrubbed clams to pan. Cook over medium heat, stirring occasionally, until all shells have opened. Discard any that do not open. Divide the pasta into warmed pasta bowls. Serve clams and sauce over pasta.

COOK'S FILE
Hints: If fresh clams are not available, use mussels, scallops or drained, tinned clams instead.

BAKED FETTUCCINE

Preparation time: 20 minutes
Total cooking time: 25 minutes
Serves 4

500 g spinach fettuccine
60 g butter or margarine
1 onion, finely chopped
300 ml carton sour cream
1 cup (250 ml) thickened or pouring
 cream

¼ teaspoon ground nutmeg
½ cup freshly grated Parmesan
 cheese
salt and freshly ground black pepper,
 to taste
1 cup freshly grated mozzarella
 cheese

1 Preheat oven to moderate 180°C.
Add fettuccine to a large pan of
rapidly boiling water and cook until
just tender. Drain well and set aside.
While pasta is cooking, melt butter
in a large pan. Add onion and stir

over low heat until onion is tender.
Add fettuccine to pan.
2 Add sour cream to pan and toss
well. Simmer, stirring, until pasta is
well coated.
3 Add cream, nutmeg, ¼ cup
Parmesan, salt and pepper; stir. Pour
into a greased casserole dish.
Sprinkle with combined mozzarella
and remaining Parmesan. Bake for
15 minutes or until cheese is
softened and golden.

SPAGHETTI MARINARA

Preparation time: 40 minutes
Total cooking time: 50 minutes
Serves 6

TOMATO SAUCE
2 tablespoons olive oil
1 onion, finely chopped
1 carrot, sliced
2 cloves garlic, crushed
425 g can crushed tomatoes
½ cup (125 ml) white wine
1 teaspoon sugar

20 black mussels
¼ cup (60 ml) white wine
¼ cup (60 ml) fish stock
1 clove garlic, crushed
375 g spaghetti
30 g butter
125 g calamari rings
125 g skinless firm white
    fish fillets, cubed
200 g raw medium prawns,
    peeled and deveined
10 g fresh flat-leaf parsley,
    chopped
200 g can clams, drained

1 For the Sauce: Heat the oil in a deep frying pan, add the onion and carrot and stir over medium heat for 10 minutes, or until the vegetables are golden. Add the garlic, tomato, wine and sugar and bring to the boil. Reduce the heat and gently simmer for 30 minutes, stirring occasionally.
2 Scrub the mussels and pull out the hairy beards. Discard any broken ones, or open ones that don't close when tapped. Rinse well. Heat the wine with the stock and garlic in a large frying pan. Add the mussels. Cover and shake the pan over high heat for 4–5 minutes. After 3 minutes, start removing opened mussels. After 5 minutes, discard any unopened mussels. Reserve the liquid.
3 Cook the spaghetti in a large pan of rapidly boiling salted water for 12 minutes, or until al dente. Drain.
4 Meanwhile, melt the butter in a frying pan, add the calamari, fish and prawns in batches and stir-fry for 2 minutes, or until just cooked through. Add the seafood to the tomato sauce with the reserved liquid, mussels, parsley and clams. Stir until the seafood is heated through. Add the spaghetti to the pan and toss until well combined.

COOK'S FILE
Note: Buy the seafood and prepare your own marinara mix, rather than buying prepared marinara mixes.

Stir-fry the calamari rings, fish and prawns until just cooked through.

After adding the seafood and liquid to the sauce, stir until heated through.

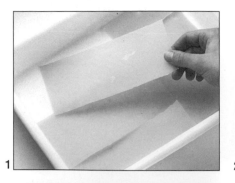

CLASSIC LASAGNE

Preparation time: 25 minutes
Total cooking time: 1 hour
15 minutes
Serves 4–6

250 g packet instant lasagne sheets
½ cup freshly grated mozzarella
cheese
½ cup freshly grated Cheddar cheese
½ cup (125 ml) thickened or pouring
cream
¼ cup grated Parmesan cheese

CHEESE SAUCE

60 g butter or margarine
⅓ cup plain flour
2 cups milk
1 cup freshly grated Cheddar cheese
salt and freshly ground black pepper,
to taste

MEAT SAUCE

1 tablespoon olive oil
1 onion, finely chopped
1 clove garlic, crushed
500 g beef mince
2 x 425 g cans tomatoes
¼ cup red wine
½ teaspoon ground oregano
¼ teaspoon ground basil
salt and freshly ground black pepper,
to taste

1 Preheat oven to moderate 180°C.
Brush a shallow oblong ovenproof
dish (approximately 24 x 30 cm)
with melted butter or oil. Line with
lasagne sheets, breaking them to fill
any gaps. Set aside.
2 To make Cheese Sauce: Melt
butter in a medium pan. Add flour
and stir for 1 minute. Remove from
heat. Gradually add milk, stirring
until mixture is smooth. Return to
heat. Cook, stirring constantly, over

medium heat until sauce boils and
thickens. Reduce heat, simmer for
3 minutes. Remove from heat, add
cheese, salt and pepper; stir until
well combined. Set aside.
3 To make Meat Sauce: Heat oil in a
large pan. Add onion and garlic and
stir over low heat until onion is
tender. Add mince. Brown well,
breaking up with a fork as it cooks.
Stir in undrained, crushed tomatoes,
wine, oregano, basil, salt and pepper.

Bring to boil. Reduce heat; simmer 20 minutes.

4 Spoon one-third of the Meat Sauce over lasagne sheets. Top with one-third of the Cheese Sauce. Arrange layer of lasagne sheets over top.

5 Continue layering, finishing with lasagne sheets. Sprinkle with combined mozzarella and Cheddar cheese.

6 Pour cream over the top. Sprinkle the lasagne with Parmesan. Bake for 35–40 minutes or until bubbling and golden.

COOK'S FILE
Note: Cheese Sauce is a variation of Bechamel Sauce. A true Bechamel uses milk infused with flavourings such as bay leaf, cloves, peppercorns, parsley sprig and cinnamon stick. To do this, bring milk to boiling point (without boiling—known as scalding) with one or more of the flavourings and allow to stand for 10 minutes before straining. To prevent the sauce forming a skin, cover surface completely with plastic wrap or greased greaseproof paper until required. Sauces are easier to handle if allowed to cool before layering.

SPAGHETTI WITH CHICKEN MEATBALLS

Preparation time: 30 minutes
+ chilling
Total cooking time: 1 hour
30 minutes
Serves 4–6

500 g (1 lb) chicken mince
60 g (2 oz) freshly grated Parmesan
2 cups (160 g/5¼ oz) fresh white
    breadcrumbs
2 cloves garlic, crushed
1 egg
freshly ground black pepper
1 tablespoon chopped fresh
    flat-leaf parsley

1 tablespoon chopped fresh sage
3 tablespoons vegetable oil

TOMATO SAUCE
1 tablespoon olive oil
1 onion, finely chopped
2 kg (4 lb) ripe tomatoes, chopped
2 bay leaves
1 cup (30 g/1 oz) fresh basil leaves,
    loosely packed
1 teaspoon coarse ground black
    pepper

500 g (1 lb) spaghetti
2 tablespoons chopped fresh
    oregano, to serve

1 In a large bowl, mix together the
mince, Parmesan, breadcrumbs,
garlic, egg, pepper and herbs. Shape

tablespoonsful of mixture into small
balls and chill for 30 minutes to firm.
Heat the oil in a shallow pan and fry
the balls in batches until golden
brown; turn often by shaking the
pan. Drain on paper towels.
2 For Tomato Sauce: Heat oil in a
large pan, add onion and fry for 1–2
minutes. Add tomato and bay leaves,
cover and bring to the boil, stirring.
Reduce heat to low, partially cover
and cook for 50–60 minutes.
3 Add meatballs, basil and pepper
and simmer for 10–15 minutes,
uncovered. Cook spaghetti in boiling
water until just tender. Drain; return
to the pan. Add some sauce to the
pasta and toss. Serve the pasta with
sauce and meatballs, sprinkled with
oregano and perhaps extra Parmesan.

Shape tablespoonsful of the mixture into small balls.

Partially cover the pan and cook for 50–60 minutes.

Add the meatballs, basil and pepper to the tomato mixture.

TAGLIATELLE WITH SWEET TOMATO AND WALNUT SAUCE

Preparation time: 20 minutes
Total cooking time: 45 minutes
Serves 4–6

4 ripe tomatoes
1 medium carrot
1 tablespoon oil
1 medium onion, finely chopped
1 stick celery, finely chopped
2 tablespoons chopped fresh parsley
1 teaspoon red wine vinegar
¼ cup white wine
salt and pepper, to taste
500 g tagliatelle or fettuccine
1 tablespoon olive oil, extra
¾ cup walnuts, roughly chopped
⅓ cup freshly grated Parmesan
  cheese, for serving

1 Mark a small cross on the bottom of each tomato. Place tomatoes in boiling water for 1–2 minutes, then plunge into cold water. Peel skin down from cross, roughly chop tomatoes. Peel and grate the carrot.
2 Heat oil in a large heavy-based pan and cook onion and celery for 5 minutes over low heat, stirring regularly. Add tomatoes, carrot, parsley and combined vinegar and wine. Reduce heat and simmer for 25 minutes. Season to taste.
3 While sauce is cooking, add pasta to a large pan of rapidly boiling water and cook until just tender. Drain and return to pan. Add sauce to pasta and toss to combine.
4 Five minutes before sauce is cooked, heat extra oil in a medium frying pan, stir walnuts over low heat for 5 minutes. Serve pasta and sauce topped with walnuts and sprinkled with Parmesan cheese.

COOK'S FILE
Hints: It is handy to have fresh parsley on hand for use in cookery so try growing your own. You'll find it grows easily in the garden or in pots.
Pasta comes in different widths and thicknesses so choose whichever type you prefer.
The Italians often use Roma or egg tomatoes when cooking sauces so try them if they are available. You'll need about 6–8 as they are small.

SPINACH AND RICOTTA CANNELLONI

Preparation time: 45 minutes
Total cooking time: 1 hour
Serves 4

FILLING
20 g butter
1 small onion, finely chopped
2 cloves garlic, crushed
3 bunches English spinach, trimmed
   and finely shredded
300 g ricotta
1 tablespoon fresh oregano

SAUCE
1 tablespoon olive oil
1 small onion, finely chopped
2 cloves garlic, crushed
440 g can peeled whole tomatoes
½ cup (125 ml) tomato pasta sauce
1 teaspoon dried oregano
2 teaspoons Dijon mustard
1 tablespoon balsamic vinegar
1 teaspoon sugar

375 g packet fresh lasagne
½ cup (75 g) grated mozzarella
½ cup (50 g) finely grated Parmesan

1 Preheat the oven to moderate 180°C (350°F/Gas 4). Cut the pasta sheets into twelve 12 cm squares. Bring a pan of salted water to the boil, blanch the lasagne in batches for 1–2 minutes, then drain flat on a damp tea towel.
2 Melt the butter in a pan and add the onion and garlic. Cook for 3–5 minutes, or until the onion softens. Add the spinach and cook for 5 minutes, or until wilted and the moisture has evaporated. Remove from the heat. Once cooled, combine with the ricotta and oregano in a food processor. Process until smooth and season.
3 To make the Sauce: Heat the oil in a pan, add the onion and garlic and cook over low heat for 8–10 minutes. Add the rest of the sauce ingredients. Bring to the boil, then reduce the heat and simmer for 10–15 minutes, or until the sauce thickens.
4 Lightly grease a 2 litre ovenproof dish. Spread one third of the sauce over the base, and then spoon 1½ tablespoons of spinach mixture onto one side of each square of lasagne, leaving a 0.5 cm border. Roll up the pasta to cover the filling and place in the dish seam-side down. Repeat with all the sheets, spacing the cannelloni evenly in the dish. Spoon in the remaining sauce and sprinkle with the cheeses. Bake for 30–35 minutes, or until the cheese is bubbling and golden. Stand for 5 minutes before serving.

Blanch the lasagne in salted boiling water in batches.

Lay the lasagne squares out flat on a clean damp tea towel to drain.

Spoon the spinach mixture onto one side of the pasta square and roll up.

ROAST SWEET POTATO RAVIOLI

Preparation time: 45 minutes
Total cooking time: 1 hour
10 minutes
Serves 6

500 g orange sweet potato, cut into
    large pieces
¼ cup (60 ml) olive oil
150 g ricotta
1 tablespoon chopped fresh basil
1 clove garlic, crushed
2 tablespoons grated Parmesan
2 x 250 g packets egg won ton
    wrappers
50 g butter
4 spring onions, sliced on the
    diagonal
2 cloves garlic, crushed, extra
300 ml cream
baby basil leaves, to serve

1 Preheat the oven to hot 220°C
(425°F/Gas 7). Place the sweet
potato on a baking tray and drizzle
with oil. Bake for 40 minutes, or
until tender.
2 Transfer the sweet potato to a bowl
with the ricotta, basil, garlic and
Parmesan and mash until smooth.
3 Cover the won ton wrappers with
a damp tea towel. Place 2 level
teaspoons of the sweet potato
mixture into the centre of one
wrapper and brush the edges with a
little water. Top with another
wrapper. Place onto a baking tray
lined with baking paper and cover
with a tea towel. Repeat with the
remaining ingredients to make 60
ravioli, placing a sheet of baking
paper between each layer.
4 Melt the butter in a frying pan.
Add the spring onion and garlic and
cook over medium heat for 1 minute.
Add the cream, bring to the boil,
then reduce the heat and simmer for
4–5 minutes, or until the cream has
reduced and thickened. Keep warm.
5 Bring a large saucepan of water to
the boil. Cook the ravioli in batches
for 2–4 minutes, or until just tender.
Drain, then divide among serving
plates. Ladle the hot sauce over the
top, garnish with basil leaves and
serve immediately.

*Drizzle the sweet potato with oil and
bake until golden.*

*Cover the filling with a won ton wrapper,
lining it up with the bottom won ton.*

*Simmer the cream mixture until it has
reduced and thickened.*

*Cook the ravioli in batches until just
tender.*

VEAL TORTELLINI WITH CREAMY SPINACH SAUCE

Preparation time: 15 minutes
Total cooking time: 20 minutes
Serves 4

500 g fresh or dried veal-filled
    tortellini
350 g frozen spinach
60 g butter

1 medium onion, chopped
1 clove garlic, crushed
½ teaspoon nutmeg
1¼ cups (300 ml) thickened or
    pouring cream
½ cup light chicken stock
salt and pepper, to taste
¼ cup grated pecorino cheese,
    to serve

1 Add pasta to a large pan of rapidly boiling water. Cook until just tender. Drain and return to pan. While pasta is cooking, allow spinach to thaw.

2 Melt butter in a heavy-based pan. Add onion and garlic; cook over low heat, stirring regularly, for 5 minutes or until golden.

3 Add drained spinach, nutmeg, cream and stock to pan. Bring to boil and simmer for 3 minutes. Add salt and pepper. Add sauce to pasta and toss to combine. Serve immediately sprinkled with pecorino cheese.

COOK'S FILE

Note: If using fresh spinach, chop the leaves; steam and add to sauce.

PASTA WITH RICOTTA, CHILLI AND HERBS

Preparation time: 15 minutes
Total cooking time: 20 minutes
Serves 4

500 g spiral pasta or penne
¼ cup olive oil
3 cloves garlic, crushed
2 teaspoons finely chopped

fresh chilli
1 cup fresh flat-leaf parsley leaves, roughly chopped
½ cup fresh basil leaves, shredded
½ cup fresh oregano leaves, roughly chopped
salt and pepper, to taste
200 g fresh ricotta cheese, cut into small cubes

1 Add pasta to a large pan of rapidly boiling water. Cook until just tender. Drain and return to pan.When pasta

is almost cooked, heat oil in a non-stick heavy-based frying pan. Add garlic and chilli to pan and stir for 1 minute over low heat.
2 Add oil mixture, herbs, salt and pepper to pasta. Toss well until mixture coats pasta thoroughly.
3 Add cubes of ricotta and serve immediately.

COOK'S FILE
Note: Fresh ricotta cheese is sold in delicatessens. Use within 2 days.

HOMESTYLE MEATBALLS WITH FUSILLI

Preparation time: 25 minutes
Total cooking time: 35 minutes
Serves 4

1 onion
750 g pork and veal mince or beef
    mince
1 cup fresh breadcrumbs
¼ cup freshly grated Parmesan
    cheese
2 tablespoons chopped fresh parsley
1 egg, beaten
1 clove garlic, crushed
rind and juice of ½ lemon
salt and freshly ground black pepper,
    to taste
¼ cup plain flour, seasoned
2 tablespoons olive oil
500 g fusilli or spiral pasta

SAUCE
425 g can tomato purée
½ cup beef stock
½ cup red wine
2 tablespoons chopped fresh basil
1 clove garlic, crushed
salt and freshly ground black pepper,
    to taste

1 Peel onion and chop very finely.
In a large bowl, combine mince,
breadcrumbs, Parmesan, onion,
parsley, egg, garlic, lemon rind and
juice, salt and pepper. Roll tablespoonsful of mixture into balls and
roll balls in seasoned flour.
2 Place oil in a large frying pan and
fry meatballs until golden. Remove
from pan, drain on paper towels. Set
aside. Remove excess fat and meat
juices from pan.
To make Sauce: In the same pan,
combine tomato puree, stock, wine,

basil, garlic, salt and pepper.
Bring to the boil.
3 Reduce heat and return meatballs
to pan. Allow to simmer for 10–15
minutes. While meatballs and sauce
are cooking, add fusilli to a large pan
of rapidly boiling water and cook

until just tender. Drain well. Serve
fusilli with meatballs and sauce over
the top.

COOK'S FILE
Hint: If liked, add 1 sliced zucchini to
sauce in step 2.

1

2

3

PASTA PIE

Preparation time: 15 minutes
Total cooking time: 55 minutes
Serves 4

250 g macaroni
1 tablespoon olive oil
1 onion, sliced
125 g pancetta, chopped
125 g ham, chopped
4 eggs
1 cup milk
1 cup (250 ml) thickened or
pouring cream
2 tablespoons snipped fresh
  chives
salt and freshly ground black
  pepper, to taste
1 cup freshly grated Cheddar
  cheese
125 g bocconcini (approximately 4),
  chopped

1 Preheat oven to moderate 180°C.
Add the macaroni to a large pan of
rapidly boiling water and cook until
just tender. Drain thoroughly. Spread
evenly over the base of a 5 cm deep
casserole dish.

2 Heat oil in a large pan. Add sliced
onion and stir over low heat until
tender. Add chopped pancetta to pan
and cook for 2 minutes. Add ham to
mixture and stir well. Remove from
heat; allow to cool.

3 In a bowl, whisk together eggs,
milk, cream, chives, salt and pepper.
Add Cheddar cheese, chopped
bocconcini and the pancetta mixture;
stir well. Spread evenly over top of
macaroni. Bake for 35–40 minutes or
until mixture is set.

COOK'S FILE
Hint: Serve with slices of egg tomato.

RIGATONI WITH KIDNEY BEANS AND ITALIAN SAUSAGE

Preparation time: 25 minutes
Total cooking time: 30 minutes
Serves 4–6

1 tablespoon olive oil
1 large onion, chopped
2 cloves garlic, crushed
4 Italian sausages, chopped
825 g can tomatoes

425 g can kidney or borlotti beans, drained
2 tablespoons chopped fresh basil
1 tablespoon chopped fresh sage
1 tablespoon chopped fresh parsley
salt and pepper, to taste
500 g rigatoni or large shells
¼ cup grated Parmesan cheese

1 Heat oil in a medium heavy-based pan. Add onion, garlic and sausage to pan and cook, stirring occasionally, over medium heat for 5 minutes.
2 Add undrained, crushed tomatoes, beans, basil, sage, parsley, salt and pepper. Reduce heat and simmer for 20 minutes.
3 While sauce is cooking, add pasta to a large pan of boiling water and cook until just tender. Drain. Divide pasta between warmed serving bowls, top with sauce. Serve immediately sprinkled with Parmesan cheese.

COOK'S FILE
Hint: If using dried beans, soak overnight in water; drain, place in a pan, cover well with water, bring to the boil and cook for 20 minutes or until tender.

PUMPKIN, BASIL AND RICOTTA LASAGNE

Preparation time: 20 minutes
Total cooking time: 1 hour
25 minutes
Serves 4

650 g pumpkin
2 tablespoons olive oil
500 g ricotta
⅓ cup (50 g) pine nuts, toasted
¾ cup (35 g) firmly packed fresh basil
2 cloves garlic, crushed
⅓ cup (35 g) finely grated Parmesan

125 g fresh lasagne sheets
1¼ cups (185 g) freshly grated mozzarella

1 Preheat the oven to moderate 180°C (350°F/Gas 4). Lightly grease a baking tray. Cut the pumpkin into 1 cm slices and arrange in a single layer on the tray. Brush with oil and cook for 1 hour, or until softened, turning halfway through cooking.
2 Place the ricotta, pine nuts, basil, garlic and Parmesan in a bowl and mix well with a wooden spoon.
3 Brush a square 20 cm ovenproof dish with oil. Cook the pasta according to the packet instructions. Arrange one third of the pasta sheets

over the base of the dish. Spread with the ricotta mixture. Top with half of the remaining lasagne sheets.
4 Arrange the pumpkin evenly over the pasta with as few gaps as possible. Season with salt and cracked black pepper and top with the final layer of pasta sheets. Sprinkle with mozzarella. Bake for 20–25 minutes, or until the cheese is golden. Leave for 10 minutes, then cut into squares.

COOK'S FILE
Note: If the pasta has no cooking instructions, blanch the sheets one at a time.

Mix together the ricotta, pine nuts, basil, garlic and Parmesan.

Cook the pasta according to the packet instructions until al dente.

Place the pumpkin on top of the lasagne sheet, leaving as few gaps as possible.

BASIC POTATO GNOCCHI

Preparation time: 30 minutes
Total cooking time: 1 hour
5 minutes
Serves 6

1 kg (2 lb) floury potatoes, unpeeled
1 egg yolk
¾ cup (90 g/3 oz) plain flour

1 Preheat the oven to moderately hot 200°C (400°F/Gas 6). Prick the unpeeled potatoes with a fork and bake for 1 hour, or until tender. Don't wrap them in foil. When cool enough to handle but still hot, peel and mash with a masher. Push through a fine sieve or process through a food mill into a bowl and make a well in the centre. Add the egg yolk, three-quarters of the flour and ½ teaspoon of salt and gradually work it in with your hands. When a loose dough forms, transfer to a lightly floured surface and knead gently with lightly floured hands. Work in the remaining flour. (If the dough is too sticky you may need to add more flour.)

2 Divide the mixture into eight portions. Roll each piece into a 20 cm (8 inch) rope. Cut the rope into 1 cm (½ inch) pieces with a floured knife. Put a piece of dough on the prongs of a fork and press down with your finger, rolling the dough as you do so. Continue with the remaining pieces. Place in a single layer on a tray lightly dusted with flour.

3 Cook the gnocchi in a large pan of boiling water for 2–3 minutes, or until they rise to the surface. Top with a sauce (see pages 14–17) and grated Parmesan.

COOK'S FILE

Storage time: Gnocchi can be frozen for up to 2 months and do not need to be thawed, but note that the cooking time will increase to 4–5 minutes.

Using a wooden spoon, push the mashed potatoes through a fine sieve.

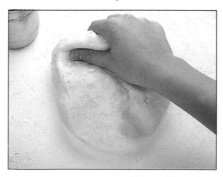

Transfer the dough to a lightly floured surface and knead gently.

Put the dough on a fork, press down with your finger and roll the gnocchi.

GNOCCHI WITH TOMATO SAUCE

Preparation time: 35 minutes
Total cooking time: 45 minutes
Serves 4

500 g potatoes, peeled and chopped
2 cups plain flour, sifted
¼ cup grated Parmesan cheese
30 g butter or margarine, melted
salt and freshly ground black pepper

2 tablespoons freshly grated
  Parmesan cheese

TOMATO SAUCE
1 kg tomatoes, peeled and chopped
2 cloves garlic, crushed
½ cup red wine
¼ cup finely chopped fresh basil
salt and freshly ground black pepper,

1 Cook potato in boiling water for 15 minutes or until soft. Drain and mash smooth. Transfer to a bowl. Add flour, cheese, butter, salt and pepper. Using a flat-bladed knife, mix to a firm dough. Knead on a lightly floured surface until smooth.
2 Roll heaped teaspoonsful of dough into oval shapes. Indent one side with the back of a fork. Cook in batches in a large pan of rapidly boiling water for 3–5 minutes. Gnocchi will float when cooked. Drain and keep warm.
3 For Tomato Sauce: Place tomatoes, garlic, wine, basil, salt and pepper in a pan. Bring to boil. Reduce heat and simmer for 15–20 minutes or until thickening. Toss gnocchi in sauce.

1

2

3

SEMOLINA GNOCCHI

Preparation time: 15 minutes
+ 1 hour refrigeration
Total cooking time: 40 minutes
Serves 4

3 cups milk
¼ teaspoon ground nutmeg
salt and freshly ground black pepper,
    to taste
⅔ cup semolina
1 egg, beaten
1½ cups grated Parmesan cheese

60 g butter or margarine, melted
½ cup thickened or pouring cream
½ cup freshly grated mozzarella
    cheese
¼ teaspoon ground nutmeg, extra

1 Line a deep 29 x 19 x 3 cm
Swiss roll tin with baking paper.
Place milk, nutmeg, salt and pepper
in a medium pan. Bring to the boil.
Reduce heat and gradually stir in
semolina. Cook, stirring occasionally,
for 5–10 minutes or until semolina is
very stiff. Remove from heat. Add
egg and 1 cup Parmesan cheese to
semolina mixture; stir to combine.

Spread mixture in prepared tin.
Refrigerate for 1 hour or until firm.
2 Preheat oven to moderate 180°C.
Cut semolina into rounds using a
floured 4 cm cutter. Arrange in a
greased shallow casserole dish.
3 Pour butter over top, followed by
cream. Sprinkle with combined
remaining Parmesan and mozzarella
cheese. Sprinkle with extra nutmeg.
Bake 20–25 minutes or until golden.

COOK'S FILE
Hint: Serve with mixed salad.

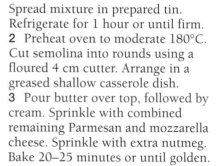

SPINACH AND RICOTTA GNOCCHI

Preparation time: 45 minutes
+ 1 hour refrigeration
Total cooking time: 15 minutes
Serves 4–6

4 slices white bread
½ cup (125 ml) milk
500 g frozen spinach, thawed
250 g ricotta
2 eggs
½ cup (50 g) grated Parmesan
¼ cup (30 g) plain flour

shaved Parmesan, to serve

GARLIC BUTTER SAUCE
100 g butter
2 cloves garlic, crushed
3 tablespoons chopped fresh basil
1 ripe tomato, diced

1 Remove the crusts from the bread and soak in milk in a shallow dish for 10 minutes. Squeeze out any excess milk from the bread. Squeeze out any excess liquid from the spinach.
2 Place the bread, spinach, ricotta, eggs and Parmesan in a bowl and mix thoroughly. Refrigerate, covered, for 1 hour. Fold the flour in well.

3 Lightly dust your hands in flour and roll heaped teaspoons of the mixture into dumplings. Lower batches of the gnocchi into a large saucepan of boiling salted water. Cook for about 2 minutes, or until the gnocchi rise to the surface. Transfer to a serving plate and keep warm.
4 To make the Garlic Butter Sauce: Combine all the ingredients in a small saucepan and cook over medium heat for 3 minutes, or until the butter is nutty brown. Drizzle over the gnocchi and sprinkle with the shaved Parmesan.

Gently squeeze out any excess milk from the bread.

With floured hands, roll teaspoons of the mixture into dumplings.

Cook the gnocchi in batches until they rise to the surface.

PIZZA, POLENTA AND RICE

PIZZA MARGHERITA

Preparation time: 25 minutes
+ 1 hour rising
Total cooking time: 45 minutes
Serves 6–8

225 g white bread flour
1 teaspoon sugar
7 g sachet dry yeast
2 tablespoons olive oil
85 ml milk

TOPPING
1 clove garlic, crushed
425 g can crushed tomatoes
1 bay leaf
1 teaspoon chopped fresh thyme
6 fresh basil leaves, chopped
150 g bocconcini, thinly sliced
olive oil, extra, to drizzle

1 Place the flour, sugar, yeast and
½ teaspoon salt in a large bowl.
Combine half the olive oil with the
milk and 85 ml warm water, and add
to the dry ingredients. Stir with a
wooden spoon to combine.
2 Place on a lightly floured work
surface and knead for 5 minutes, or
until soft and smooth. Lightly oil a
bowl, add the dough and turn to coat
in the oil. Leave in a warm place
for 1 hour, or until doubled in size.
Preheat the oven to hot 210°C
(415°F/Gas 6–7).
3 Meanwhile, heat the remaining oil
in a saucepan over medium heat, add
the garlic and cook, stirring, for
30 seconds. Add the tomato, bay leaf,
thyme and basil and simmer, stirring
occasionally, for 20–25 minutes, or
until thick and fragrant. Allow to
cool. Remove the bay leaf.
4 Place the dough on a lightly floured
work surface, then punch down to
expel the air and knead for 5 minutes.
Shape the dough into a neat ball and
roll out to a 28–30 cm diameter.
Lightly oil a 28–30 cm pizza tray and
place the dough on the tray. Spread
the tomato sauce over the dough,
leaving a 3 cm border. Arrange the
bocconcini over the sauce, drizzle
with olive oil and bake for 15 minutes,
or until crisp and bubbling.

COOK'S FILE
Note: The red, white and green
toppings of this pizza symbolise
the Italian flag.

*Roll the pizza dough out to a 28–30 cm
diameter.*

*Arrange the bocconcini slices over the
tomato sauce.*

HAM AND CHEESE CALZONI

Preparation time: 30 minutes
+ chilling
Total cooking time: 30 minutes
Makes 4

2 cups (250 g/8 oz) plain flour
100 g (3⅓ oz) butter, chopped
2 egg yolks

HAM AND CHEESE FILLING
250 g (8 oz) ricotta cheese
50 g (1⅔ oz) Gruyère cheese, cubed
50 g (1⅔ oz) ham, finely chopped

2 spring onions, chopped
1 tablespoon chopped fresh
    flat-leaf parsley
freshly ground black pepper

1 Lightly grease a large oven tray. Sift the flour and a pinch of salt into a bowl and rub in the butter. Make a well in the centre, cut in the egg yolks with a knife and add 2–3 tablespoons water, or enough to form a dough. Gather together into a ball, cover with plastic wrap and chill for 20 minutes. Preheat the oven to moderately hot 200°C (400°F/Gas 6).
2 To make Filling: Combine the cheeses, ham, spring onions, parsley and black pepper in a bowl.

3 Roll out a quarter of the dough to make a large round 2–3 mm (⅛ inch) thick, trimming any uneven edges. Spoon a quarter of the filling mixture into the centre, brush the edge very lightly with water and fold over to enclose the filling, pressing the edge to seal. Repeat with the remaining dough and filling. Place the Calzoni on the oven tray, brush with a little olive oil and bake for 30 minutes, or until well browned and crisp.

COOK'S FILE
Note: Calzoni can be made 1 day ahead and kept refrigerated before baking. Pastry can be made in a food processor, in short bursts.

Use a knife to cut the egg yolks into the flour and butter.

Mix together the cheeses, ham, spring onions, parsley and pepper in a bowl.

Brush the edge of the pastry with water, then fold over to enclose the filling.

FETA, TOMATO AND OLIVE PIZZA

Preparation time: 30 minutes
+ 1 hour rising
Total cooking time: 50 minutes
Serves 4–6

7 g sachet dry yeast
¾ cup (90 g) plain flour
¾ cup (110 g) wholemeal plain flour
1 tablespoon olive oil

TOPPING
1 tablespoon oil
2 onions, sliced
2 teaspoons soft brown sugar
1–2 tablespoons olive paste
250 g cherry tomatoes, halved
200 g feta, crumbled
¼ cup (7 g) loosely packed fresh basil, shredded

1 To make the dough, place the yeast and flours in a large bowl and mix well. Make a well in the centre and add the olive oil and ½ cup (125 ml) warm water. Mix well, adding a little more water if the dough seems too dry, then gather together with your hands. Turn out onto a lightly floured surface and knead for 5 minutes. Place the dough into a lightly oiled bowl, cover with plastic wrap and leave in a draught-free place for 1 hour.

2 Meanwhile, heat the oil in a frying pan and cook the onion over medium–low heat for 20 minutes, stirring regularly. Add the sugar and cook, stirring, for 1–2 minutes, or until caramelised. Set aside to cool.

3 Preheat the oven to hot 220°C (425°F/Gas 7). Punch down the dough and knead for 1 minute. Roll out to a 30 cm round (it will shrink as you roll it), then tuck 1 cm of the dough under to create a rim. Sprinkle an oven tray lightly with polenta or brush with oil, and place the dough on the tray.

4 Spread the paste over the dough, leaving a 1 cm border, then top with the onion. Arrange the tomato halves over the onion, and sprinkle with feta and basil. Bake for 25 minutes.

Pour the olive oil and ½ cup (125 ml) warm water into the well.

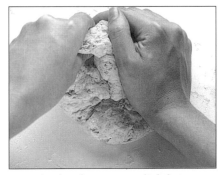

Turn the dough out onto a lightly floured surface and knead.

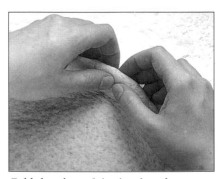

Fold the edges of the dough under to make a rim.

Sprinkle the feta over the onion and tomato.

POTATO ONION PIZZA

Preparation time: 40 minutes
Total cooking time: 40 minutes
Serves 4

7 g (¼ oz) sachet dry yeast
½ teaspoon sugar
1½ cups (185 g/6 oz) plain flour
1 cup (150 g/4¾ oz) wholemeal plain
    flour
1 tablespoon olive oil

TOPPING
1 large red capsicum
1 potato, peeled
1 large onion, sliced
125 g (4 oz) soft goats cheese
3 tablespoons capers
1 tablespoon dried oregano
1 teaspoon cracked pepper
1 teaspoon olive oil

1 Mix the yeast, sugar, a good pinch of salt and 1 cup (250 ml/8 fl oz) warm water in a bowl. Cover with plastic wrap and leave in a warm place for 10 minutes, or until foamy. Sift both flours into a bowl. Make a well in the centre, add the yeast mixture and mix to a firm dough. Knead on a lightly floured surface for 5 minutes, or until smooth. Roll out to a 35 cm (14 inch) round. Brush a 30 cm (12 inch) tray with oil; put the dough on the tray and tuck the edge over to form a rim. Preheat oven to moderately hot 200°C (400°F/Gas 6).

2 To make Topping: Cut the capsicum into large flat pieces; remove the seeds. Place, skin-side-up, under a hot grill until blackened. Cool under a tea towel, peel away the skin and cut the flesh into narrow strips.
3 Slice the potato paper thin and arrange on the base with the onion and capsicum. Crumble on half the goats cheese. Sprinkle with capers, oregano and pepper and drizzle with olive oil. Brush the edge of the crust with oil and bake for 20 minutes. Crumble on remaining goats cheese and bake for 15–20 minutes, or until crust has browned. Cut into wedges.

COOK'S FILE
Note: Goats cheese, also known as Chèvre, is available at delicatessens.

Tuck the edge of the pizza dough over to form a rim.

Remove the skin from the capsicum and cut the flesh into thin strips.

Arrange the onion, capsicum and half the goats cheese over the base.

PIZZA-TOPPED FOCACCIA

Preparation time: 30 minutes
+ 1 hour 30 minutes standing
Total cooking time: 40 minutes
Serves 4

7 g (¼ oz) dried yeast
1 teaspoon sugar
2 tablespoons olive oil
2½ cups (310 g/10 oz) plain flour,
　sifted

TOPPING
1 tablespoon tomato paste
1 large red capsicum,
　thinly sliced
125 g (4 oz) marinated artichoke
　hearts, quartered
¼ cup (30 g/1 oz) black olives, pitted
200 g (6½ oz) bocconcini, thickly
　sliced

1 Combine the yeast, ¾ cup (185 ml/ 6 fl oz) of warm water and the sugar in a bowl and set aside in a warm place for 5–10 minutes, or until frothy. Put the oil, flour and 1 teaspoon salt in a large bowl, add the frothy yeast and mix to a soft dough.
2 Turn the dough out onto a lightly floured surface and knead for 10 minutes, or until smooth and elastic. Form into a ball and place in a large oiled bowl. Cover with oiled plastic wrap and set aside in a warm place for 1 hour, or until doubled in size.
3 Preheat the oven to moderate 180°C (350°F/Gas 4). Punch down the dough with your fist to expel any air, and knead for 1 minute. Roll into a flat disc large enough to fit into a greased 23 cm (9 inch) springform

tin. Press into the tin, cover with a tea towel and leave to rise for about 20 minutes.
4 Spread the tomato paste over the dough, and arrange the other topping ingredients, except for the bocconcini, on top. Bake for 20 minutes, remove from the oven

and spread the slices of bocconcini over the top, then bake for a further 20 minutes, or until the dough is well risen and firm to the touch in the centre. Cool on a wire rack before cutting and serving.

Cut the bocconcini into thick slices with a sharp knife.

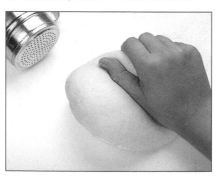

On a lightly floured surface, knead the dough until smooth and elastic.

Arrange the capsicum, artichokes and olives over the tomato paste.

CALZONE WITH OLIVES, CAPERS AND ANCHOVIES

Preparation time: 35 minutes
+ 1 hour 45 minutes rising
Total cooking time: 15 minutes
Serves 4

1 tablespoon caster sugar
7 g sachet dry yeast
4⅓ cups (540 g) plain flour
3 tablespoons olive oil
polenta, for dusting

FILLING
2 tablespoons olive oil
200 g mozzarella cheese, cut into
   1 cm cubes
2 medium tomatoes, juice squeezed
   out and cut into 1 cm dice
12 basil leaves, roughly torn into
   pieces
20 pitted black olives
2 teaspoons baby capers
12 anchovy fillets, cut into thin strips
   2 cm long

1 Place the sugar, yeast and ⅓ cup (80 ml) warm water in a small bowl. Leave in a warm place for 15 minutes, or until foamy. If it does not foam in 5 minutes the yeast is dead and you must start again.
2 Sift the flour into a large bowl with ½ teaspoon salt. Add the yeast mixture, olive oil and ⅔ cup (170 ml) warm water. Mix with a wooden spoon until the dough loosely clumps together. Turn it out onto a lightly floured surface and knead to form a soft, moist but non-sticky dough. Add a little extra flour or warm water as needed. Knead for 15–20 minutes, or until smooth and

elastic, and a finger imprint springs straight out.
3 Oil the sides of a large bowl with olive oil. Roll the ball of dough around in the bowl to coat the surface with oil, then cut a shallow cross on the top of the ball with a sharp knife. Cover the bowl with a tea towel and leave in a warm place for up to 1 hour 30 minutes, or until the dough has doubled in size.
4 Preheat the oven to very hot 230°C (450°F/Gas 8). Lightly oil 2 pizza or baking trays and dust with polenta. Punch down the dough and place it on a lightly floured work surface. Divide the dough into two portions. One or both portions can be frozen at this stage for future use. Shape one portion into a ball. Roll it out to a circle of roughly 25 cm. Using the heels of your hands and working from the centre outwards, press the circle to a diameter of 32 cm. Transfer the dough to the tray. Brush the surface lightly with olive oil.
5 Scatter half the mozzarella over one half of the dough, leaving a 1 cm border at the outer edge. Scatter half the tomato and basil over the cheese, and season well with salt and freshly ground black pepper. Distribute half the olives, capers and anchovies over the top. Fold the undressed half of dough over the filling to form a half-moon shape. Press the edges together firmly to seal. Turn the cut edge up and over on itself and press into a scroll pattern to further seal in the filling. Brush the surface with a little more olive oil. Repeat the process with the remaining ingredients to make a second calzone. Bake for 10–15 minutes, or until puffed and golden brown.

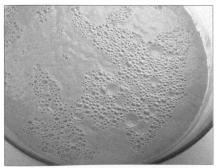

Leave the yeast, sugar and water mixture in a warm place until foamy.

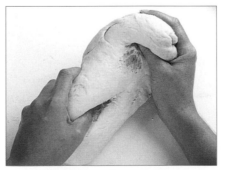

Knead the dough to form a soft, moist but non-sticky dough.

Place the dough on a lightly floured work surface and divide in half.

Press the dough out to a 32 cm diameter circle with the heels of your hands.

Distribute half the filling ingredients over the dough.

Press the edges together in a scroll pattern to fully seal.

Dissolve the sugar in the water, add the yeast and leave until frothy.

Cook the onions in the oil until they are soft and golden.

Knead the dough on a floured surface for about 10 minutes, until smooth.

Spread the cooked onion over the pizza base and then scatter with olives.

OLIVE AND ONION PIZZA

Preparation time: 25 minutes
Total cooking time: 35–40 minutes
Serves 4–6

1 teaspoon sugar
1½ teaspoons dried yeast
½ cup (125 ml/4 fl oz) olive oil
5 onions, thinly sliced
1 cup (125 g/4 oz) self-raising flour
½ cup (125 g/4 oz) plain white flour
1 cup (185 g/6 oz) black olives
2 tablespoons grated Parmesan cheese

1 Dissolve the sugar in ½ cup (125 ml/ 4 fl oz) warm water. Sprinkle with yeast and leave for 10 minutes, or until frothy.
2 Heat 3 tablespoons oil in a frying pan and fry the onion for 10 minutes, or until soft. Leave to cool. Preheat the oven to hot 220°C (425°F/Gas 7).
3 Sift together the self-raising flour, plain flour and a good pinch of salt in a bowl. Make a well in the centre and pour in the yeast mixture and 2 tablespoons oil. Bring together to form a dough and knead on a lightly floured surface for 10 minutes, or until smooth. Extra flour may be necessary.
4 Roll out the dough to line a greased 30 cm (12 inch) tray. Spread

with cooked onions, then olives. Brush the crust with remaining olive oil. Bake for 25–30 minutes. Serve hot or cold, sprinked with Parmesan.

ROASTED TOMATO AND EGGPLANT PIZZA

Preparation time: 40 minutes
Total cooking time: 1 hour
45 minutes
Serves 4

500 g (1 lb) plum tomatoes
1 large eggplant
olive oil, for frying
200 g (6½ oz) mozzarella, grated
¼ cup (25 g/¾ oz) grated Parmesan
1 tablespoon chopped fresh oregano

PIZZA BASE
1 teaspoon dried yeast
¼ teaspoon salt
¼ teaspoon sugar
1¼ cups (155 g/5 oz) plain flour
6 cloves garlic, crushed

1 Preheat the oven to slow 150°C (300°F/Gas 2). Cut the tomatoes in half and place in one layer on a baking tray, cut-side-up. Sprinkle with salt and roast for 1 hour 15 minutes. Set aside to cool.
2 To make Pizza Base: Put the yeast, salt, sugar and ½ cup (125 ml/4 fl oz) warm water in a small bowl. Leave, covered with plastic wrap, in a warm place for 10 minutes, or until foamy. Sift the flour into a large bowl, make a well in the centre and add the yeast mixture and garlic. Mix to form a dough. Knead on a lightly floured surface for 10 minutes, or until smooth and elastic. Roll out to fit a 30 cm (12 inch) greased or non-stick pizza tray.
3 Preheat the oven to moderately hot 200°C (400°F/Gas 6). Thinly slice the eggplant. Drizzle a char-grill or large frying pan with olive oil until nearly smoking. Add the eggplant in batches and cook, turning once, until soft (brush the eggplant with a little more oil if it starts to stick). Drain on paper towels.
4 Arrange the eggplant on the pizza base. Top with tomatoes and sprinkle with the combined mozzarella and Parmesan. Bake for 20–30 minutes, or until the base is cooked and the cheese melted and golden. Sprinkle with fresh oregano to serve.

Cut the tomatoes in half and sprinkle with sea salt.

Make a well in the centre of the flour and add the yeast and garlic.

Cook the eggplant in batches, turning once, until soft.

Put the eggplant on the pizza base and top with the tomatoes.

PIZZETTAS

SUN-DRIED TOMATO PESTO AND ARTICHOKE

Preheat the oven to moderately hot 200°C (400°F/ Gas 6). To make Pesto: Place ½ cup (75 g/2½ oz) whole sun-dried tomatoes, 2 tablespoons pine nuts, 2 cloves of garlic and 2 tablespoons grated Parmesan cheese in a food processor. Process until smooth. Divide the pesto among 4 individual pizza bases. Slice 4 marinated artichoke hearts and place on top of the pesto. Sprinkle with 1 cup (150 g/4¾ oz) grated mozzarella cheese. Bake for 15–20 minutes, or until the base is crisp and the cheese has melted. Serves 4.

BOCCONCINI AND TOMATO

Preheat the oven to moderately hot 200°C (400°F/Gas 6). Combine 3 tablespoons olive oil with 8 crushed cloves of garlic. Drizzle the mixture over 4 individual pizza bases. Bake for 10 minutes. Slice 4 egg tomatoes and place on the pizza bases. Top with 4 sliced fresh bocconcini, cracked black pepper and salt. Return to the oven and cook for a further 6 minutes, or until the cheese has melted. Sprinkle pizzettas with ½ cup (30 g/1 oz) shredded basil. Serves 4.

CHAR-GRILLED CAPSICUM AND PROSCIUTTO

Preheat the oven to moderately hot 200°C (400°F/ Gas 6). Spread 1 cup (250 g/8 oz) ready-made pizza sauce over 4 individual pizza bases. Cut 1 red and 1 green capsicum into large, flattish pieces and place, skin-side-up, under a hot grill. Cook until the skin blackens and blisters. Remove from the heat and cover with a tea towel; leave to cool. Peel away the skin and cut the flesh into thin strips. Divide among the pizza bases. Cut 12 thin slices of prosciutto into strips and place on top of the capsicum. Top the prosciutto with ⅔ cup (125 g/4 oz) good-quality black olives, pitted and sliced. Drizzle with extra virgin olive oil. Bake for 10–15 minutes, or until the crusts are golden. Serves 4.

SWEET POTATO AND SCALLOP

Preheat the oven to moderately hot 200°C (400°F/Gas 6). Drizzle 4 individual pizza bases with olive oil. Clean and cut in half 250 g (8 oz) scallops and arrange on the bases. Very thinly slice 375 g (12 oz) sweet potato and deep-fry until golden and crisp; drain well. Thinly slice 1 red onion. Top the scallops with sweet potato and onion and drizzle with extra virgin olive oil. Bake for 10–15 minutes. Sprinkle with 2 tablespoons chopped fresh thyme to serve. Serves 4.

HERBED TOMATO AND ROCKET

Preheat the oven to moderately hot 200°C (400°F/Gas 6). Heat 1 tablespoon olive oil in a pan. Add 1 finely chopped onion and 2 crushed cloves of garlic and cook over medium heat for 3–4 minutes. Peel and chop 500 g (1 lb) ripe egg tomatoes and add to the pan with 2 tablespoons chopped fresh herbs. Cook over high heat for 5–7 minutes, or until the mixture is quite thick; spread over 4 individual pizza bases. Bake for 10–15 minutes, or until the bases are crisp. Remove from the oven and top with 2 cups (40 g/1⅓ oz) torn rocket leaves. Sprinkle with shavings of Parmesan and season with cracked black pepper. Serves 4.

CARAMELISED ONION AND GOATS CHEESE

Preheat the oven to moderately hot 200°C (400°F/Gas 6). Slice 4 onions very finely. Heat 2 tablespoons olive oil in a large pan; cook the onion over high heat for 2–3 minutes, or until starting to brown. Reduce the heat and cook for 15 minutes, or until the onion is soft. Spread the onion over 4 individual pizza bases. Top with 125 g (4 oz) goats cheese, crumbled or thinly sliced. Bake for 10–15 minutes, or until the crusts are golden. Remove from the oven and sprinkle with 2 tablespoons chopped fresh oregano. Serves 4.

Pizzettas from left: Sun-dried Tomato Pesto and Artichoke; Bocconcini and Tomato; Char-grilled Capsicum and Prosciutto; Sweet Potato and Scallop; Herbed Tomato and Rocket; Caramelised Onion and Goats Cheese

VEGETABLE AND POLENTA PIE

Preparation time: 20 minutes
+ 15 minutes standing
+ refrigeration
Total cooking time: 50 minutes
Serves 6

2 eggplants, thickly sliced
1⅓ cups (350 ml) vegetable stock
1 cup (150 g) fine polenta
½ cup (50 g) finely grated Parmesan
1 tablespoon olive oil
1 large onion, chopped
2 cloves garlic, crushed
1 large red capsicum, cut into
    1 cm cubes
2 zucchini, thickly sliced
150 g button mushrooms, cut into
    quarters
400 g can chopped tomatoes
3 teaspoons balsamic vinegar
olive oil, for brushing

1 Spread the eggplant in a single layer on a board, and sprinkle with salt. Leave for 15 minutes, then rinse, pat dry and cut into cubes.
2 Line a 22 cm round cake tin with foil. Pour the stock and 1⅓ cups (350 ml) water into a saucepan and bring to the boil. Add the polenta in a thin stream and stir over low heat for 5 minutes, or until the liquid is absorbed and the mixture is thick and comes away from the side of the pan.
3 Remove from the heat and stir in the cheese until it melts all through the polenta. Spread into the prepared tin, smoothing the surface as much as possible. Refrigerate until set.
4 Preheat the oven to moderately hot 200°C (400°F/Gas 6). Heat the

oil in a large saucepan with a lid and add the onion. Cook over medium heat, stirring occasionally, for 3 minutes, or until soft. Add the garlic and cook for a further 1 minute. Add the eggplant, capsicum, zucchini, mushrooms and tomato. Bring to the boil, then reduce the heat and simmer, covered, for 20 minutes, or until the vegetables are tender. Stir occasionally to prevent catching on the bottom of the pan. Stir in the vinegar and season.

5 Transfer the vegetable mixture to a 22 cm ovenproof pie dish, piling it up slightly in the centre.
6 Turn out the polenta, peel off the foil and cut into 12 wedges. Arrange smooth-side-down in a single layer, over the vegetables—don't worry about any gaps. Brush lightly with a little olive oil and bake for 20 minutes, or until lightly brown and crisp.

Cook the polenta, stirring, until all the liquid is absorbed and it is very thick.

Reduce the heat and simmer until the vegetables are tender.

Arrange the polenta wedges, smooth-side-down, over the vegetable mixture.

POLENTA SQUARES WITH WILD MUSHROOMS

Preparation time: 25 minutes
+ 20 minutes refrigeration
+ 10 minutes standing
Total cooking time: 40 minutes
Serves 4

2 cups (500 ml) vegetable stock
1 cup (150 g) medium-grain polenta
20 g butter
¾ cup (75 g) grated Parmesan
5 g dried porcini mushrooms
200 g Swiss brown mushrooms
300 g field mushrooms
½ cup (125 ml) olive oil
1 onion, chopped
3 cloves garlic, finely chopped
1 fresh bay leaf
2 teaspoons chopped fresh thyme
2 teaspoons chopped fresh oregano
½ cup (15 g) finely chopped fresh flat-
    leaf parsley
1 tablespoon balsamic vinegar
¼ cup (25 g) grated Parmesan, extra

1 Place the stock and a pinch of salt in a large saucepan and bring to the boil. Add the polenta in a steady stream, stirring constantly. Reduce the heat and simmer, stirring occasionally, for 15–20 minutes. Remove from the heat and stir in the butter and Parmesan.
2 Grease a 20 cm square shallow cake tin, spread the mixture into the tin and refrigerate for 20 minutes.
3 Place the porcini mushrooms in a bowl and cover with ½ cup (125 ml) boiling water. Leave for 10 minutes, or until softened. Drain, reserving ⅓ cup (80 ml) liquid. Wipe the mushrooms with a damp cloth to remove any dirt. Thickly slice the Swiss brown mushrooms, and coarsely chop the field mushrooms. Heat ⅓ cup (80 ml) olive oil in a large frying pan, add the mushrooms and cook for 4–5 minutes. Remove from the pan. Heat the remaining oil in the pan, add the onion and cook over medium heat for 2–3 minutes, or until transparent.
4 Add the reserved soaking liquid, garlic, bay leaf, thyme and oregano, season and cook for 1 minute. Return the mushrooms to the pan and add the parsley and balsamic vinegar, and cook over medium heat for 1 minute. Remove the bay leaf.
5 Sprinkle the extra Parmesan over the polenta and place under a medium grill for 10 minutes, or until lightly brown and the cheese has melted. Cut into four 10 cm squares.
6 Place a polenta square in the centre of each serving plate and top with the mushroom mixture. Season with freshly ground black pepper.

Spread the polenta mixture into the prepared cake tin.

Add the chopped parsley and balsamic vinegar to the mushroom mixture.

Sprinkle Parmesan over the polenta and grill until the cheese has melted.

Add the polenta to the stock and water and stir constantly until very thick.

Use the back of a spoon to spread the polenta in the tin.

Build up the layers of sliced polenta, butter and cheese.

Add the final layer of sliced polenta and then sprinkle with Parmesan cheese.

BAKED POLENTA WITH THREE CHEESES

Preparation time: 20 minutes
+ 2 hours chilling
Total cooking time: 45 minutes
Serves 4

POLENTA
2½ cups (600 ml/20 fl oz) chicken
    stock
2 cups (300 g/9⅔ oz) polenta
½ cup (50 g/2⅔ oz) freshly grated
    Parmesan

CHEESE FILLING
100 g (3⅓ oz) havarti cheese, sliced
100 g (3⅓ oz) mascarpone
100 g (3⅓ oz) blue cheese, crumbled
100 g (3⅓ oz) butter, sliced thinly
½ cup (50 g/1⅔ oz) freshly grated
    Parmesan

1 To make Polenta: Brush a 7-cup (1.75 litre) loaf tin with oil. Put the stock and 2 cups (500 ml/16 fl oz) water in a large pan and bring to the boil. Add the polenta and stir for 10 minutes until very thick.
2 Remove from the heat and stir in the Parmesan. Spread into the tin and smooth the surface. Refrigerate for 2 hours, then cut into about 30 thin slices. Preheat the oven to moderate 180°C (350°F/Gas 4).
3 Brush a large ovenproof dish with oil. Place a layer of polenta slices on the base. Top with a layer of half the combined havarti, mascarpone and blue cheeses and half the butter. Add another layer of polenta and top with the remainder of the three cheeses and butter. Add a final layer of polenta and sprinkle the Parmesan on top. Bake for 30 minutes, or until a golden crust forms. Serve immediately.

COOK'S FILE
Note: Polenta is also known as cornmeal and is available from most supermarkets and delicatessens.

ARANCINI
(Rice Croquettes)

Preparation time: 45 minutes
+ 10 minutes soaking
+ 1 hour refrigeration
Total cooking time: 1 hour
Makes 10

2 cups (440 g/14 oz) short-grain rice
1 egg, lightly beaten
1 egg yolk
½ cup (50 g/1¾ oz) grated Parmesan

MEAT SAUCE
1 dried porcini mushroom
1 tablespoon olive oil
1 onion, chopped
125 g (4 oz) minced beef or veal
2 slices prosciutto, finely chopped
2 tablespoons tomato paste
⅓ cup (80 ml/2¾ fl oz) white wine
½ teaspoon dried thyme leaves
3 tablespoons finely chopped fresh
    parsley

plain flour
2 eggs, lightly beaten
dry breadcrumbs, for coating
oil, for deep-frying

1 Cook the rice in boiling water for 20 minutes, or until just soft. Drain, without rinsing, and cool. Put in a large bowl and add the egg, egg yolk and Parmesan. Stir until the rice sticks together. Cover and set aside.
2 To make the Meat Sauce: Soak the mushroom in hot water for 10 minutes to soften, then squeeze dry and chop finely. Heat the oil in a frying pan. Add the mushroom and onion and cook for 3 minutes, or until soft. Add the mince and cook, stirring, until it is browned. Now add the prosciutto, tomato paste, wine, thyme and pepper to taste. Cook, stirring, for 5 minutes, or until all the liquid has been absorbed. Stir in the parsley and set aside to cool.
3 With wet hands, form the rice mixture into 10 balls. Wet your hands again and gently pull the balls apart. Place 3 teaspoons of the meat sauce in the centre of each. Reshape to enclose the filling. Roll in the flour, beaten egg and breadcrumbs and chill for 1 hour.
4 Fill a deep heavy-based pan one third full of oil and heat until a cube of bread browns in 15 seconds. Deep-fry the croquettes in oil, two at a time, for 3–4 minutes, or until golden brown. Drain on paper towels and keep warm while cooking the rest.

Soak the dried mushroom in hot water, then squeeze dry and chop finely.

Gently pull the balls of rice apart and fill with 3 teaspoons of meat sauce.

Reshape the balls and roll them in the flour, egg and breadcrumbs.

SEAFOOD RISOTTO

Preparation time: 30 minutes
Total cooking time: 40 minutes
Serves 4 (6 as an entrée)

12 baby clams
1½ cups (375 ml) white wine
3½ cups vegetable stock
2 bay leaves
1 celery stick, chopped
6 French shallots, chopped
¼ cup (60 ml) lemon juice
12 raw king prawns, peeled and
    deveined
12 scallops without roe, beards
    removed
1 calamari tube, cut into 12 slices
1 tablespoon olive oil
2 tablespoons butter
⅔ cup (80 g) chopped spring
    onion
4–6 cloves garlic, crushed
1½ tablespoons finely chopped
    fresh thyme
1½ cups (330 g) arborio rice
⅓ cup (90 g) sour cream
⅓ cup (35 g) grated Parmesan
2 tablespoons chopped fresh
    flat-leaf parsley
shaved Parmesan, to serve

1   Scrub and rinse the clams to remove any grit, discarding any that are opened or damaged. Place the wine, stock, bay leaves, celery, shallots, lemon juice and 2½ cups (625 ml) water in a saucepan and bring to the boil for 5 minutes. Reduce the heat to a simmer, then add the clams and cook for 3 minutes, or until they open. Using a slotted spoon, transfer the clams to a bowl, discarding any that did not open. Add the prawns to the stock and cook for 2 minutes, or until pink and curled, then transfer to the bowl with the clams. Add the scallops and calamari rings and cook for 1 minute, then transfer to the bowl. Strain the stock, then return to the pan and keep at a low simmer.

2   Heat the oil and half the butter in a large heavy-based saucepan over medium heat. Add the spring onion, garlic and thyme and cook, stirring, for 1 minute. Stir in the rice and cook for 1 minute, or until well coated.

3   Add ½ cup (125 ml) of the hot stock. Stir constantly over medium heat until all the stock is absorbed. Continue adding more stock, ½ cup (125 ml) at a time, stirring constantly for 25 minutes, or until the stock is absorbed. Add the seafood with the final addition of stock. The rice should be tender and creamy.

4   Remove from the heat and stir in the sour cream, Parmesan and parsley. Season. Serve with shaved Parmesan.

Cook the clams in the simmering stock until they open.

Cook the prawns until they are pink and curled.

Stir constantly until the stock has been absorbed.

LEMON AND HERB RISOTTO WITH FRIED MUSHROOMS

Preparation time: 30 minutes
Total cooking time: 45 minutes
Serves 4

RISOTTO
1 litre chicken or vegetable stock
pinch saffron threads
2 tablespoons olive oil
2 leeks, thinly sliced
2 cloves garlic, crushed
2 cups (440 g) arborio rice
2–3 teaspoons finely grated lemon
    rind
2–3 tablespoons lemon juice
2 tablespoons chopped fresh
    flat-leaf parsley
2 tablespoons snipped fresh chives
2 tablespoons chopped fresh
    oregano
70 g grated Parmesan cheese
100 g mascarpone

FRIED MUSHROOMS
30 g butter
1 tablespoon virgin olive oil
200 g small flat mushrooms, cut into
    thick slices
1 tablespoon balsamic vinegar

1 Bring the stock and saffron threads to the boil in a large saucepan. Reduce the heat, cover and keep at a low simmer.
2 Heat the olive oil in a large saucepan over medium heat. Add the leek, cook for 5 minutes, then add the garlic and cook for a further 5 minutes, or until golden. Add the rice and stir for 1 minute, or until well coated with the oil.
3 Add half the lemon rind and juice, then add ½ cup (125 ml) of the hot stock. Stir constantly over medium heat until all the liquid has been absorbed. Continue adding more stock, ½ cup (125 ml) at a time, stirring constantly, for 25 minutes, or until the stock is absorbed and the rice is tender and creamy.
4 Stir in the parsley, chives, oregano, Parmesan, mascarpone and the remaining lemon rind and lemon juice, then remove from the heat, cover and keep warm.

5 To cook the mushrooms, melt the butter and virgin olive oil in a large frying pan, then add the mushroom slices and vinegar and cook, stirring, over high heat for 5–7 minutes, or until the mushrooms are tender and all the liquid has been absorbed.
6 Serve the risotto in large bowls topped with the mushrooms. Garnish the risotto with sprigs of fresh herbs, if desired.

Stir the leek and garlic until the leek is lightly golden.

Stir constantly until the stock is absorbed and the rice is creamy.

95

ASPARAGUS AND PISTACHIO RISOTTO

Preparation time: 10 minutes
Total cooking time: 30 minutes
Serves 4–6

1 litre vegetable stock
1 cup (250 ml) white wine
⅓ cup (80 ml) extra virgin olive oil
1 red onion, finely chopped
2 cups (440 g) arborio rice
310 g asparagus spears, trimmed and cut into 3 cm pieces
½ cup (125 ml) cream
1 cup (100 g) grated Parmesan
½ cup (40 g) shelled pistachio nuts, toasted and roughly chopped

1 Heat the stock and wine in a large saucepan, bring to the boil, then reduce the heat, cover and keep at a low simmer.
2 Heat the oil in another large saucepan. Add the onion and cook over medium heat for 3 minutes, or until soft. Add the rice and stir for 1 minute, or until the rice is translucent.
3 Add ½ cup (125 ml) hot stock, stirring constantly over medium heat until the liquid is absorbed. Continue adding more stock, ½ cup (125 ml) at a time, stirring constantly for 20–25 minutes, or until all the stock is absorbed and the rice is tender and creamy in texture. Add the asparagus during the last 5 minutes of cooking. Remove from the heat.
4 Stand for 2 minutes, stir in the cream and Parmesan and season to taste with salt and black pepper. Serve sprinkled with pistachios.

Add the rice to the saucepan and stir until it is translucent.

Add a little more stock when most of the liquid has been absorbed.

Stir the cream and Parmesan through the risotto.

PUMPKIN RISOTTO

Preparation time: 25 minutes
Total cooking time: 1 hour
Serves 4–6

600 g pumpkin, cut into
   1 cm cubes
3 tablespoons olive oil
2 cups (500 ml) vegetable stock
1 onion, finely chopped
2 cloves garlic, finely chopped
1 tablespoon chopped fresh
   rosemary
2 cups (440 g) arborio rice
½ cup (125 ml) white wine
30 g butter
⅓ cup (35 g) grated Parmesan cheese
3 tablespoons finely chopped fresh
   flat-leaf parsley

1 Preheat the oven to moderately hot 200°C (400°F/Gas 6). Toss the pieces of pumpkin in 2 tablespoons of the oil, place in a baking dish and roast for 30 minutes, or until tender and golden. Turn the pumpkin pieces halfway through the cooking time.
2 Heat the stock and 3 cups (750 ml) water in a saucepan, cover and keep at a low simmer.
3 Heat the remaining oil in a large saucepan, and cook the onion, garlic and rosemary, stirring, over low heat for 5 minutes, or until the onion is cooked but not browned. Add the rice and stir to coat. Stir in the wine for 2–3 minutes, or until absorbed.
4 Add ½ cup (125 ml) stock, stirring constantly over medium heat until all the liquid is absorbed. Continue adding stock ½ cup (125 ml) at a time, stirring constantly for 20 minutes, or until all the stock is absorbed and the rice is tender and creamy. Season to taste with salt and freshly ground black pepper and stir in the pumpkin, butter, Parmesan and parsley. Serve immediately.

Add the wine to the rice and stir until absorbed.

Gradually add the stock to the rice until it is all absorbed and the rice is tender.

Stir the pumpkin, butter, Parmesan and parsley through the rice.

FISH AND SEAFOOD

INSALATA DI FRUTTI DI MARE
(Seafood salad)

Preparation time: 45 minutes
+ 40 minutes marinating
Total cooking time: 10 minutes
Serves 4

500 g small calamari
1 kg large clams
1 kg black mussels
500 g raw medium prawns,
peeled, deveined, tails intact
5 tablespoons finely chopped
fresh flat-leaf parsley

DRESSING
2 tablespoons lemon juice
⅓ cup (80 ml) olive oil
1 clove garlic, crushed

1 Grasp the body of the calamari in one hand and the head and tentacles in the other. Gently pull apart to separate. Cut the tentacles from the head by cutting below the eyes. Discard the head. Push out the beak and discard. Pull the quill from inside the body of the calamari and discard. Under cold running water, pull away all the skin (the flaps can be used). Rinse well, then slice the calamari into 7 mm rings.

2 Scrub the clams and mussels and remove the beards. Discard any shellfish that are cracked or don't close when tapped. Rinse under cold running water. Fill a large saucepan with 2 cm water, add the clams and mussels, cover, bring to the boil and cook for 4–5 minutes, or until the shells open. Remove, reserving the liquid. Discard any that do not open. Remove the mussels and clams from their shells and place in a large bowl.

3 Pour 1 litre water into the pan, bring to the boil and add the prawns and calamari. Cook for 3–4 minutes, or until the prawns turn pink and the calamari is tender. Drain and add to the clams and mussels.

4 To make the Dressing: Combine the lemon juice, olive oil and garlic in a small bowl and whisk together. Season with salt and freshly ground black pepper. Pour the dressing over the seafood, add 4 tablespoons of the parsley and toss to coat. Adjust the seasoning if necessary. Cover and marinate in the refrigerator for 30–40 minutes to allow the flavours to develop. Sprinkle with remaining parsley and serve with slices of fresh crusty bread.

Remove the transparent quill from inside the body of the calamari.

Gently pull the mussels and clams out of their shells.

CHARGRILLED TUNA WITH CAPONATA

Preparation time: 25 minutes
+ 1 hour standing + cooling
Total cooking time: 50 minutes
Serves 6

CAPONATA
500 g ripe tomatoes
750 g eggplant, cut into 1 cm cubes
⅓ cup (80 ml) olive oil
2 tablespoons olive oil, extra
1 onion, chopped
3 celery sticks, chopped
2 tablespoons drained capers
½ cup (90 g) green olives, pitted
1 tablespoon sugar
½ cup (125 ml) red wine vinegar

olive oil, for brushing
6 x 200 g tuna steaks

1 To make the Caponata: Score a cross in the base of each tomato. Place in a bowl of boiling water for 1 minute, then plunge into cold water and peel away from the cross. Cut into 1 cm cubes.
2 Sprinkle the eggplant with salt and leave for 1 hour. Place in a colander, rinse under cold running water and pat dry. Heat half the oil in a frying pan, add half the eggplant and cook for 4–5 minutes, or until golden and soft. Remove. Repeat with the remaining oil and eggplant. Remove.
3 Heat the extra oil in the same pan, add the onion and celery, and cook for 3–4 minutes, or until golden. Reduce the heat to low, add the tomato and simmer for 15 minutes, stirring occasionally. Stir in the capers, olives, sugar and vinegar, season and simmer, stirring occasionally, for 10 minutes, or until slightly reduced. Stir in the eggplant. Remove from the heat and cool.
4 Heat a chargrill plate and brush lightly with olive oil. Cook the tuna for 2–3 minutes each side, or until cooked to your liking. Serve immediately with the Caponata.

Cook the eggplant in two batches until golden and soft.

Add the capers, olives, sugar and vinegar to the tomato mixture.

Cook the tuna on a chargrill plate until cooked to your liking.

HERBED WHOLE SALMON

Preparation time: 15 minutes
Total cooking time: 35 minutes
Serves 6–8

1 teaspoon fennel seeds
2 tablespoons extra virgin olive oil
2 cloves garlic, finely chopped
¾ cup (60 ml) white wine
¾ teaspoon sugar
1 teaspoon chopped fresh dill
2 kg whole salmon, scaled
　and cleaned
1 lemon, sliced
¾ cup (10 g) fresh dill sprigs

1　Preheat the oven to moderately hot 190°C (375°F/Gas 5). Place the fennel seeds in a dry frying pan and roast over high heat for 30–60 seconds or until fragrant; do not burn. Grind in a spice grinder to form a fine powder. Whisk in a bowl with the olive oil, garlic, wine, sugar and chopped dill.

2　Pat the fish dry with paper towels and make 2 diagonal cuts in the thickest part of the fish on each side. Season, then stuff lemon slices and dill sprigs into the cavity. Place enough foil to cover the fish on a lined baking tray. Place the fish on top and pour on the wine mixture. Wrap loosely and bake for 30–35

minutes, or until the dorsel fin pulls away easily or the fish flakes easily when tested with a fork (salmon should be rare in the centre so it is moist).

3　Cut with a spoon on the natural marking along the fish, then across in sections and pull away from the bone (remove the skin if you like). Serve with melted butter mixed with lemon juice and juices from the fish.

Push the lemon slices and dill sprigs into the salmon cavity.

Put the fish on a serving plate and cut along the natural line with a spoon.

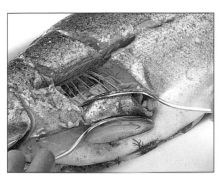

Cut sections across the fish with the spoon and pull away from the bone.

Remove the clear quills from inside the calamari and purple skin from outside.

Add the breadcrumbs, parsley and Parmesan and mix until well combined.

Divide the filling among the calamari tubes but don't fill them completely.

Shallow-fry the calamari in batches for 3–4 minutes on each side.

STUFFED CALAMARI

Preparation time: 30 minutes
Total cooking time: 20 minutes
Serves 4

8 medium calamari tubes
40 g (1⅓ oz) butter
8 slices pancetta, finely chopped
400 g (12⅔ oz) raw prawns, peeled, deveined and finely chopped
1 cup (80 g/2⅔ oz) fresh breadcrumbs
¼ cup (10 g/⅓ oz) chopped fresh parsley
1 cup (100 g/3⅓ oz) grated Parmesan
100 g (3⅓ oz) butter, extra
3 cloves garlic, crushed
1 tablespoon chopped fresh parsley, extra

1 Rinse the calamari under cold water. Put your hand in and remove the insides and quill. Then remove the purple skin from the outside. Rinse and pat dry with paper towels.
2 Melt the butter in a small frying pan; cook the pancetta and prawns over high heat until the prawns are just cooked. Transfer to a bowl; add the breadcrumbs, parsley and Parmesan and mix well.
3 Divide the filling among the calamari tubes. Melt the extra butter with the garlic in a large frying pan and cook the stuffed calamari, in batches, for 3–4 minutes on each side, or until just cooked. Stir through the extra parsley. Place two stuffed calamari on each plate and spoon over a little of the garlic butter.

COOK'S FILE
Note: Only three-quarters fill the calamari tubes—they shrink when cooked and the filling will ooze out if overfilled.

MUSSELS IN TOMÁTO AND HERB SAUCE

Preparation time: 30 minutes
Total cooking time: 35 minutes
Serves 4

TOMATO AND HERB SAUCE
⅓ cup (80 ml) olive oil
3 cloves garlic, finely chopped
¼ teaspoon dried chilli flakes
2 x 425 g cans crushed tomatoes
1 teaspoon caster sugar

8 slices crusty Italian bread
2 tablespoons olive oil
2 large cloves garlic, halved
1 kg black mussels
2 tablespoons olive oil, extra
1 red onion, finely chopped
6 sprigs fresh flat-leaf parsley
2 sprigs fresh thyme
2 sprigs fresh oregano
1 cup (250 ml) dry white wine
1 tablespoon chopped fresh flat-leaf
   parsley
2 teaspoons fresh thyme leaves
2 teaspoons chopped fresh oregano
   leaves

1 Preheat the oven to warm 160°C (315°F/Gas 2–3). To make the Tomato Sauce: Heat the oil in a saucepan, add the garlic and chilli flakes, and cook over low heat for 30 seconds without browning. Add the tomato, sugar and ⅓ cup (80 ml) water. Season and simmer, stirring often, for 15 minutes, or until reduced and thickened.
2 Lightly brush the bread with olive oil. Place in a single layer on a baking tray and bake for 10 minutes, or until crisp and golden. While still warm, rub one side with the garlic.
3 Meanwhile, scrub the mussels with a stiff brush and pull out the hairy beards. Discard any broken mussels or ones that don't close when tapped on a bench. Rinse well.
4 Heat the extra oil in a large saucepan, add the onion and cook over medium heat for 3 minutes, or until softened but not browned. Add the parsley, thyme, oregano and wine. Bring to the boil, then reduce the heat and simmer for 5 minutes. Season with pepper.

5 Add the mussels, stir to coat, and cook, covered, for 3–4 minutes. Shake the pan often. Remove the mussels as they open. Discard any unopened mussels.
6 Strain the wine mixture into the tomato sauce, discarding the onion and herbs. Return to the large saucepan and reheat. Add the

mussels and toss well to coat in the mixture. Pile into a serving bowl and scatter with the chopped parsley, thyme and oregano. Arrange the bread slices around the bowl.

Pull the hairy beards out of the scrubbed mussels.

Remove the mussels as they open and discard any that don't open.

BAKED FISH WITH GARLIC BREADCRUMBS

Preparation time: 15 minutes
Total cooking time: 20 minutes
Serves 4

4 fillets firm white fish
   (about 200 g/6½ oz each)
75 g (2½ oz) butter, melted
3 cloves garlic, crushed
2 cups (160 g/5¼ oz) fresh white
   breadcrumbs

(made from Italian bread)
1 tablespoon finely chopped parsley
lemon wedges, to serve

1 Preheat the oven to moderately hot 200°C (400°F/Gas 6). Brush an ovenproof dish with olive oil and arrange the fish in a single layer.
2 Mix together the butter and garlic in a bowl and set aside. Mix together the breadcrumbs and parsley and scatter in a thick layer over the fish. Drizzle with the garlic butter.
3 Bake for 20 minutes, or until the fish is white and flakes easily and the

crumbs are golden brown. If the crumbs are not golden but the fish is cooked, flash under a hot grill for a couple of minutes. Don't take your eyes off it as it can burn very quickly. Serve with lemon wedges.

COOK'S FILE
Note: Fresh breadcrumbs are very simple to make. Remove the crusts from slightly stale (at least one-day old) slices of bread. Put the bread in a food processor and mix until crumbs form. Use ordinary bread or, as in this recipe, Italian bread.

Brush an ovenproof dish with olive oil and arrange the fish in a single layer.

Mix together the fresh breadcrumbs and parsley and scatter over the fish.

Bake until the fish is white and can be easily flaked with a fork.

FISH IN PARCHMENT

Preparation time: 20 minutes
Total cooking time: 20 minutes
Serves 4

4 deep sea perch fillets (about
   150–200 g/5–6 oz each)
1 leek, white part only, cut into
   julienne strips (see Note)
4 spring onions, cut into julienne
   strips
2 teaspoons finely chopped chives

30 g (1 oz) butter
1 lemon, cut into 12 very thin slices
juice of 1 lemon, extra

1 Preheat the oven to moderate 180°C (350°F/Gas 4). Place each fish fillet in the centre of a piece of baking paper large enough to enclose the fish.
2 Scatter over the leek, spring onion and chives. Top each with a teaspoon of butter and 3 slices of lemon. Squeeze over the extra lemon juice. Bring the top and bottom edges of the paper together and fold over,

then scrunch over the sides to make a parcel. Put on a baking tray and bake for 20 minutes.
3 Check to see that the fish is cooked (it should be white and easily flaked with a fork) and then serve. You can either let each person open their own parcel or take out the fish with an egg slice and serve on warm plates. Good with mixed wild and brown rice.

COOK'S FILE
Note: Julienne strips are thin, regular, matchstick-sized pieces of vegetables. They cook quickly and look attractive.

Slice the leek and the spring onions very finely to make julienne strips.

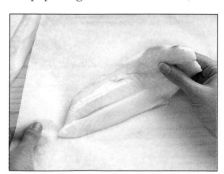

Place each fish fillet in the centre of a piece of baking paper.

Scatter over the julienne vegetables and top with butter and lemon slices.

Baked Fish with Garlic Breadcrumbs (top) and Fish in Parchment

BAKED TROUT WITH FENNEL AND WATER CHESTNUTS

Preparation time: 20 minutes
Total cooking time: 20–30 minutes
Serves 4

4 whole small trout, cleaned and gutted
1 tablespoon sea salt
1 teaspoon cracked black pepper
2 fennel bulbs, trimmed and thinly sliced
230 g (7⅓ oz) canned water chestnuts, drained
½ cup (125 ml/4 fl oz) fresh lemon juice
½ cup (125 ml/4 fl oz) dry white wine

1 Preheat oven to moderate 180°C (350°F/Gas 4). Arrange trout, side by side, in a large baking dish, and sprinkle with sea salt and pepper.
2 Top with the sliced fennel and water chestnuts. Pour over the lemon juice and wine and cover with foil.
3 Bake for 20–30 minutes, or until the fish flakes with a fork and the fennel is tender, then remove the foil and serve immediately.

Trim the stalk and base from the fennel bulbs and thinly slice.

Arrange the trout, side-by-side, in a dish and sprinkle with salt and pepper.

Top the trout with fennel and chestnuts, then pour over the lemon juice and wine.

FRITTO MISTO DI MARE
(Fried seafood salad)

Preparation time: 20 minutes
Total cooking time: 10 minutes
Serves 4

200 g cuttlefish
800 g red mullet fillets
½ teaspoon paprika
75 g plain flour
12 raw medium prawns,
   peeled, deveined, tails intact
good-quality olive oil,
for deep-frying
lemon wedges, to serve

1 Preheat the oven to slow 150°C (300°F/Gas 2). Line a large baking tray with baking paper. Place the cuttlefish bone-side-down on a board and, using a sharp knife, gently cut lengthways through the body. Open out, remove the cuttlebone and then gently remove the insides. Cut the flesh in half. Under cold running water, pull the skin away. Cut the cuttlefish and mullet into even-size pieces. Pat dry well with paper towels. Season with salt and freshly ground black pepper. Mix the paprika and flour together in a bowl, add the seafood and toss to coat. Shake off any excess flour.

2 Fill a deep heavy-based saucepan one third full of oil and heat to 190°C (375°F), or until a cube of bread dropped in the oil browns in 10 seconds. Add the seafood in batches and cook for 1 minute, or until golden and cooked through. Drain on crumpled paper towels. Keep warm on the baking tray in the oven while you cook the rest.

3 Place all the seafood on a serving platter. Sprinkle with extra salt and serve with lemon wedges.

Using a sharp knife, gently cut lengthways through the cuttlefish body.

Remove the cuttlebone and the insides from the cuttlefish.

Add the seafood to the flour and paprika mixture and toss to coat.

Cut open the octopus heads and discard the guts.

Remove the beaks from the octopus and cut the tentacles into sections.

Toss the octopus over high heat until it becomes opaque.

When most of the liquid has evaporated add the tomato and onions.

OCTOPUS IN FRESH TOMATO SAUCE

Preparation time: 20 minutes
Total cooking time: 1 hour
10 minutes
Serves 4–6

1 kg (2 lb) baby octopus
2 tablespoons olive oil
⅓ cup (80 ml/2¾ fl oz) dry white wine
500 g (1 lb) ripe tomatoes, peeled and chopped
4 pickling onions and quartered
1 clove garlic, chopped
2 tablespoons chopped fresh flat-leaf parsley

1 Wash the octopus and cut the heads off. Cut open the heads and remove the guts. Wash the heads and drain. Remove the beaks and cut the tentacles into sets of four.
2 Heat the oil in a large pan until very hot, add the octopus and toss over high heat for about 10 minutes, or until the octopus is opaque and the pan almost dry. Add the wine and simmer, uncovered, until most of the liquid has evaporated, then add the tomato and onions. Bring to the boil, then reduce the heat and simmer over low heat for 45 minutes to 1 hour, or until tender.
3 Serve hot or warm, sprinkled with the combined chopped garlic and parsley and lots of black pepper.

CREAMY FISH STEW

Preparation time: 15 minutes
Total cooking time: 20 minutes
Serves 4

500 g pappardelle pasta
50 g butter
4 cloves garlic, crushed
150 g oyster mushrooms
800 g raw medium prawns,
    peeled and deveined
2 x 400 g salmon fillets,
    skin removed, cut into
    2.5 cm cubes
1 cup (250 ml) white wine
1 cup (250 ml) fish stock
¼ teaspoon saffron threads

400 ml crème fraîche
125 g sugar snap peas
    or snow peas

1 Cook the pasta in a large saucepan of rapidly boiling salted water for 12 minutes, or until *al dente*. Drain and keep warm.
2 Meanwhile, melt the butter in a large deep frying pan, add the garlic and oyster mushrooms and cook for 1 minute. Add the prawns and salmon and cook for a further 2–3 minutes, or until the prawns are cooked and the salmon starts to flake but is still rare in the centre. Be careful not to burn the garlic. Transfer to a bowl.
3 Pour the wine and stock into the pan and add the saffron. Scrape the

base of the pan to remove sediment. Bring to the boil, then reduce the heat and simmer rapidly for 5 minutes, or until reduced by half. Add the crème fraîche and sugar snap peas and stir through. Bring to the boil, then reduce the heat and simmer, stirring occasionally, for 3–4 minutes, until the liquid has slightly thickened.
4 Return the seafood mixture and any juices to the pan and gently stir over medium heat until warmed through. Divide the pasta among four plates and spoon the seafood and sauce over it. Season, to taste, and serve immediately.

Cook the mushrooms, garlic, prawns and salmon until the fish just starts to flake.

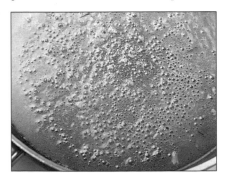

Add the wine, stock and saffron to the pan. Scrape the sediment from the base.

Simmer the mixture, stirring occasionally, until the sauce has slightly thickened.

WHITEBAIT FRITTERS

Preparation time: 20 minutes
+ resting
Total cooking time: 15 minutes
Makes 10

¼ cup (30 g/1 oz) self-raising flour
¼ cup (30 g/1 oz) plain flour
½ teaspoon bicarbonate of soda
1 teaspoon salt
freshly ground black pepper

1 egg, lightly beaten
3 tablespoons dry white wine
2 teaspoons chopped fresh
   flat-leaf parsley
1 clove garlic, crushed
½ small onion, grated
200 g (6½ oz) whitebait
olive oil, for shallow frying
lemon wedges, to serve

1 Sift the flours, bicarbonate of soda, salt and pepper into a bowl. Stir through the egg and wine, whisk until smooth, then add the parsley, garlic, onion and whitebait. Cover and leave for 20 minutes.

2 Heat the oil in a frying pan and then drop in tablespoons of batter. When the batter is puffed and bubbles appear on the surface, carefully turn to cook the other side.

3 Drain on paper towels and serve immediately with lemon wedges.

Add the parsley, garlic, onion and whitebait, cover and leave for 20 minutes.

Heat the oil in a frying pan, then drop in tablespoons of batter.

Cook both sides of the fritters, then lift out of the pan and drain on paper towels.

SARDINES WITH HERB AND PARMESAN CRUST

Preparation time: 40 minutes
+ 30 minutes refrigeration
Total cooking time: 40 minutes
Serves 4

1½ cups (120 g) fresh
    breadcrumbs
½ cup (50 g) grated Parmesan
3 tablespoons chopped fresh
    flat-leaf parsley
2 eggs
12 butterflied fresh sardines
½ cup (125 ml) light olive oil,
    for pan-frying

TOMATO AND OLIVE SAUCE
1 tablespoon olive oil
1 small onion, finely chopped
2 cloves garlic, finely chopped
410 g bottle tomato pasta sauce
1 cup (250 ml) chicken stock
1 teaspoon sugar
½ cup (75 g) pitted black olives,
    chopped
2 tablespoons chopped fresh basil

1 Mix the breadcrumbs, Parmesan and parsley in a bowl. Lightly beat the eggs in a separate bowl. Dip the sardines in the egg, drain off any excess, then coat with breadcrumb mixture. Place in a single layer on a tray or plate and chill for 30 minutes.
2 For the Tomato and Olive Sauce: Heat the oil in a saucepan, add the onion and garlic and cook over medium heat for 2–3 minutes, or until the onion is soft. Add the tomato sauce, stock and sugar. Bring to the boil, then reduce the heat and simmer, stirring occasionally, for 20 minutes, or until the sauce has thickened. Stir in the olives and basil.
3 Heat the light olive oil in a large frying pan, add the sardines and cook in batches for 2–3 minutes each side, or until golden brown and cooked through. Serve with the sauce.

Coat the sardines with the breadcrumb mixture and refrigerate for 30 minutes.

Meanwhile, for the tomato and olive sauce, finely chop the small onion.

Simmer the sauce until thickened, stirring occasionally with a wooden spoon.

Cook the sardines in batches until golden brown and cooked through.

SALMON WITH TOMATO FENNEL DRESSING

Preparation time: 20 minutes
Total cooking time: 25 minutes
Serves 4

2 ripe tomatoes
1 kg King Edward potatoes, chopped
100 g butter
100 ml milk or cream, warmed
1 tablespoon chopped fresh chervil
1 tablespoon chopped fresh
   tarragon
⅓ cup (80 ml) olive oil
2 spring onions, finely chopped
1 bulb baby fennel, finely chopped
1 tablespoon baby capers
2 tablespoons red wine vinegar
4 salmon fillets or ocean trout
   fillets, skin on (150 g each)

1 Score a cross in the base of the tomatoes, place in a heatproof bowl and cover with boiling water. Leave for 10 seconds, then transfer to cold water and peel the skin away from the cross. Cut in half and scoop out the seeds with a teaspoon. Chop.
2 Cook the potatoes in a large saucepan of boiling water for 15 minutes, or until soft. Drain well and return to the heat until all the moisture has been absorbed. Remove from the heat and mash smooth. Add the butter and gradually beat in the milk with a wooden spoon. Stir in the herbs, season, cover and keep warm.
3 Meanwhile, heat 1 tablespoon of the oil in a large frying pan, add the spring onion and fennel and cook over medium heat for 10 minutes, or until very soft, then add the tomato, capers and vinegar and bring to the

boil for 1 minute. Do not overcook or the tomatoes will go mushy. Remove from the heat and keep warm.
4 Pat the fillets dry with paper towels and rub the skin with a little salt. Heat the remaining oil in a large frying pan, add the fillets, skin-side-down, and cook over medium heat for 2–3 minutes, or until very crisp,

then turn and cook for 2 minutes for a medium–rare result.
5 Serve, skin-side-up, on a bed of mash with the dressing. (The dressing may soften the skin if served on top.)

Peel the skin away from the cross at the base of the tomato.

Cut the tomatoes in half and scoop the seeds out with a teaspoon.

Cook the fillets until the skin is crisp, then turn and cook the other side.

GRILLED CALAMARI WITH SALSA VERDE

Preparation time: 30 minutes
+ 30 minutes marinating
Total cooking time: 15 minutes
Serves 4

1 kg calamari
1 cup (250 ml) olive oil
2 tablespoons lemon juice
2 cloves garlic, crushed
2 tablespoons chopped fresh oregano
2 tablespoons chopped fresh
    flat-leaf parsley
6 lemon wedges

SALSA VERDE
2 anchovy fillets, drained
1 tablespoon capers
1 clove garlic, crushed
2 tablespoons chopped fresh
    flat-leaf parsley
2 tablespoons olive oil

1   To clean the calamari, hold onto the hood and gently pull the tentacles away from the head. Cut out the beak and discard with any intestines still attached to the tentacles. Rinse the tentacles in cold running water, pat dry and cut into 5 cm lengths. Place in a bowl. Clean out the hood cavity and remove the transparent backbone. Under cold running water, pull away the skin, rinse and dry well. Cut into 1 cm rings and place in the bowl with the tentacles. Add the oil, lemon juice, garlic and oregano to the bowl, and toss to coat the calamari. Refrigerate for 30 minutes.
2   To make the Salsa Verde: Crush the anchovy fillets in a mortar and pestle or in a bowl with a wooden spoon.

Rinse the capers and dry with paper towels. Chop the capers very finely and add to the anchovies. Add the garlic and parsley, then slowly stir in the olive oil. Season with black pepper and salt, if necessary (the anchovies may be very salty). Mix well.
3   Drain the calamari and cook on a hot barbecue or grill in 4 batches for

1–2 minutes each side, basting with the marinade. To serve, sprinkle the calamari with salt, pepper and fresh parsley, and serve with the Salsa Verde and lemon wedges.

Hold the calamari and gently pull the tentacles away from the head.

Combine the anchovies, capers, garlic and parsley.

Cook the calamari in batches on a hot barbecue or grill.

Once the mussels have cooled a little, remove them from their shells.

Mix the tomato paste with water and whisk into the simmering liquid.

Gradually add the milk, stirring constantly over low heat until thickened.

Spoon the White Sauce over the mussels and Tomato Sauce.

MUSSELS IN TWO SAUCES

Preparation time: 25 minutes
Total cooking time: 45 minutes
Serves 4

3 tablespoons olive oil
1.25 kg (2½ lb) mussels in shells, scrubbed

TOMATO SAUCE
2 cloves garlic, crushed
½ cup (125 ml/4 fl oz) white wine
3 tablespoons tomato paste

WHITE SAUCE
25 g (¾ oz) butter
¼ cup (30 g/1 oz) plain flour
1 cup (250 ml/8 fl oz) milk
3 tablespoons grated mozzarella
2 tablespoons grated Parmesan

1 Heat half the oil in a large pan. Add the mussels and cook over high heat, shaking the pan, for 5 minutes until opened. Discard any that do not open. Strain the liquid and reserve. Let the mussels cool, then remove from their shells. Preheat the oven to moderately hot 190°C (375°F/Gas 5).
2 To make Tomato Sauce: Heat the remaining oil in a pan. Add the garlic and fry until golden. Add the wine and reserved liquid and simmer gently for 5 minutes. Mix the tomato paste with 3 tablespoons water, then whisk into the simmering liquid. Simmer for a further 10 minutes and season to taste with salt and pepper.
3 To make White Sauce: Melt the butter in a pan. Add the flour and cook for 1 minute. Very gradually stir in the milk over low heat until the sauce thickens. Season.
4 Combine the Tomato Sauce and mussels and pour into four 1-cup (250 ml/8 fl oz) ramekins. Spoon over the White Sauce. Sprinkle with the combined cheeses and bake for 20 minutes. Serve with crusty bread.

TROUT WITH LEEK AND CAPER SAUCE

Preparation time: 10 minutes
Total cooking time: 10 minutes
Serves 4

45 g (1½ oz) melted butter
4 thick ocean trout fillets
(about 155 g/5 oz each)

LEEK AND CAPER SAUCE
50 g (1⅔ oz) butter
1 leek, chopped
1 cup (250 ml/8 fl oz) white wine
(riesling or chardonnay)
2 tablespoons capers, drained
1 tablespoon chopped flat-leaf
parsley

1 Brush a shallow oven tray with melted butter and put the fish on the tray. Brush with melted butter and grill under moderate heat, without turning, until the fish is just cooked.

Remove and cover loosely with foil to keep warm while making the sauce.
2 To make Leek and Caper Sauce: Melt the butter in a pan and cook the leek gently until soft, but not brown. Add the wine and simmer for 3–4 minutes. Add the capers and parsley and salt and pepper to taste, then remove from the heat.
3 Spoon the hot sauce over the fish.

COOK'S FILE
Variation: Use salmon fillets or cutlets or any thick white fish instead of trout.

Cut down the sides of the leek (not all the way to the base) to wash thoroughly.

Brush the trout with melted butter and grill until almost cooked.

Add the capers, parsley, salt and pepper, then remove from the heat.

PAN-FRIED FISH

Preparation time: Nil
Total cooking time: 8 minutes
Serves 4

plain flour, for dusting
olive oil
4 white fish steaks (swordfish or cod)

1 Sift the flour together with a little salt and pepper onto a dinner plate. Coat both sides of the fish with seasoned flour; shake off the excess.
2 Heat about 3 mm (⅛ inch) oil in a frying pan until very hot. Put the fish into the hot oil and cook for 3 minutes on one side, then turn and cook the other side for 2 minutes, or until the coating is crisp and well browned. Reduce the heat to low and cook for a further 2–3 minutes, until the flesh flakes easily with a fork.
3 Remove from the pan and drain briefly on paper towels, then serve straight away, perhaps with lemon wedges, sautéed potatoes and a salad.

COOK'S FILE
Note: Cook the fish in batches, if necessary. Don't overcrowd the pan or the temperature will be reduced.

Coat both sides of the fish with seasoned flour and shake off the excess.

Cook the fish for 3 minutes, then turn over. Cook in batches if necessary.

Remove from the pan and drain briefly on paper towels.

PARMESAN PRAWNS

Preparation time: 30 minutes
+ 15 minutes refrigeration
Total cooking time: 10 minutes
Serves 6

1 kg raw king prawns
1 cup (125 g) plain flour, seasoned
2 eggs, lightly beaten
1½ cups (150 g) dry breadcrumbs
½ cup (50 g) grated Parmesan
1 tablespoon finely chopped fresh
    flat-leaf parsley
light olive oil, for deep-frying
100 g mixed salad greens

TOMATO SALSA
1 tablespoon extra virgin olive oil
1 tablespoon lime juice
2 cloves garlic, crushed
3 small Roma tomatoes, peeled,
    seeded and finely diced
10 black olives, pitted, chopped
1 tablespoon finely shredded
    fresh basil
1 tablespoon capers, finely chopped
2 tablespoons whole-egg
    mayonnaise

1 Peel the prawns, leaving the tails intact. Gently pull out the dark vein from each prawn back, starting at the head end.
2 Measure the flour into a bowl and put the eggs in a separate bowl. Mix the breadcrumbs, Parmesan, parsley and salt and pepper, to taste, in another bowl.
3 Add the prawns to the flour, in batches, and lightly toss to coat, shaking off any excess. Dip into the egg, then roll in the breadcrumbs, pressing the crumbs on firmly.

Place on a tray and refrigerate, uncovered, for 15 minutes.
4 For the Tomato Salsa, whisk the oil, lime juice and garlic together in a bowl. Stir in the tomato, olives, basil, capers, mayonnaise, and salt and pepper, to taste.
5 Fill a deep saucepan one third full of oil and heat to 180°C (350°F), or until a cube of bread dropped in the

oil browns in 15 seconds. Deep-fry batches of prawns for 1–2 minutes, or until golden. Drain on crumpled paper towels.
6 For serving, arrange the prawns over some of the salad greens. Season with salt and pepper, to taste. Serve with the Tomato Salsa.

Toss the prawns in flour, dip in the egg, then press firmly in the breadcrumbs.

Mix the oil, juice and garlic, then stir in the remaining salsa ingredients.

When the prawns are golden and cooked through, remove with a slotted spoon.

MEAT AND CHICKEN

OLIVE AND LEMON LAMB CUTLETS

Preparation time: 15 minutes
+ marinating
Total cooking time: 10 minutes
Serves 4

12 lamb cutlets
2 tablespoons olive oil
juice and zest of 1 lemon
1 clove garlic, crushed
1 teaspoon finely chopped fresh
   rosemary leaves
1 teaspoon butter
16 black olives, cut into strips
2 tablespoons chopped parsley

1 Trim the lamb cutlets of fat and place in a dish. Pour over 1 tablespoon of the oil, the lemon juice and zest, garlic and chopped rosemary. Leave to marinate for at least 30 minutes.
2 Heat the remaining oil and the butter in a large frying pan. Drain the cutlets, reserving the marinade, and fry over medium heat until cooked through, turning once. Remove from the pan and set aside.
3 Drain the excess fat from the pan and add the olives, parsley and remaining marinade. Bring to the boil and cook for 2 minutes. Season to taste with salt and pepper, pour over the cutlets and serve with mashed or roasted potatoes.

Trim the fat away from the lamb cutlets, leaving just the meat and bone.

Pour over 1 tablespoon of oil, the lemon juice and zest, garlic and rosemary.

Fry the cutlets over medium heat until they are cooked through, turning once.

Add the olives, parsley and remaining marinade and cook for 2 minutes.

SPRING CHICKEN WITH HONEY GLAZE

Preparation time: 15 minutes
Total cooking time: 55 minutes
Serves 6–8

2 small (1.5 kg/3 lb) chickens
1 tablespoon light olive oil

HONEY GLAZE
3 tablespoons honey
juice and finely grated rind of 1 lemon

1 tablespoon finely chopped
  rosemary
1 tablespoon dry white wine
1 tablespoon white wine vinegar
2 teaspoons Dijon mustard
1½ tablespoons olive oil

1 Preheat the oven to moderate 180°C (350°F/Gas 4). Halve the chickens by cutting down either side of the backbone. Discard the backbones. Cut the chickens into quarters; brush with oil and season lightly. Place on a rack in a roasting pan, skin-side-down, and roast for 20 minutes.

2 To make Honey Glaze: Combine all the ingredients in a small pan. Bring to the boil, reduce the heat and simmer for 5 minutes.
3 After cooking one side, turn the chickens over and baste well with the warm glaze. Return to the oven and roast for 20 minutes. Baste once more and cook for a further 15 minutes. Serve hot or cold.

COOK'S FILE
Note: To test if the chicken is cooked, pierce the meat at its thickest point. The juices should run clear.

Halve each chicken by cutting down either side of the backbone.

Cut the chickens into quarters—you will find kitchen scissors easier than a knife.

Cook one side of the chicken, then turn over and baste with warm glaze.

VEAL SCALOPPINI WITH LEMON SAUCE

Preparation time: 5 minutes
Total cooking time: 5 minutes
Serves 4

3 tablespoons olive oil
60 g (2 oz) butter
8 thin veal steaks
plain flour, for coating

2 tablespoons lemon juice
2 tablespoons finely chopped parsley
lemon slices, to garnish

1 Heat the oil and half the butter in a large frying pan until quite hot. Coat the veal steaks in the flour and add to the pan, cooking in batches if necessary. Cook until lightly browned on one side, then turn over and brown the other side. The veal steaks should take only 1 minute on each side—cooking longer will toughen the meat. Transfer to a warm plate and season with salt and pepper.
2 Lower the heat and add the lemon juice, parsley and remaining butter to the pan, stirring to combine. Add the veal steaks, turning them in the sauce.
3 Serve the veal steaks with the sauce. Garnish with lemon slices.

COOK'S FILE
Note: For thin veal steaks, cover them with plastic wrap and beat with a rolling pin or meat mallet.

Coat the veal steaks in flour, shaking off any excess.

Lightly brown the veal steaks on either side, cooking in batches if necessary.

Return all the veal steaks to the pan, turning to coat them in sauce.

BEEF WITH PROSCIUTTO AND MUSHROOMS

Preparation time: 15 minutes
Total cooking time: 25 minutes
Serves 4

2 tablespoons olive oil
200 g (6½ oz) button mushrooms, stalks trimmed
60 g (2 oz) sliced prosciutto, cut into wide strips
4 thick slices beef scotch fillet or eye fillet steaks
2 cloves garlic, crushed
2 tablespoons chopped fresh flat-leaf parsley
¼ cup (60 ml/2 fl oz) dry white wine
½ cup (125 ml/4 fl oz) cream

1 Preheat the oven to moderately hot 200°C (400°F/Gas 6). Heat the oil in a deep ovenproof frying pan (large enough to hold the beef steaks in one layer, without overlapping). Add the mushrooms and prosciutto and toss until the mushrooms start to brown.

2 Layer the steaks over the mushrooms, sprinkle with garlic and parsley, then pour over the wine. Bring to the boil, reduce the heat, then cover the pan (with a lid or tightly with foil) and bake for 10–15 minutes, or until the steaks are cooked to taste.
3 Set the steaks aside to keep warm. Heat the pan on the hotplate, add the cream and boil for 3–5 minutes, or until thickened slightly; pour over the steaks and serve immediately.

Add the mushrooms and prosciutto to the oil and toss until starting to brown.

Sprinkle the steaks with garlic and parsley and then pour in the wine.

Add the cream to the pan and boil for 3–5 minutes, or until slightly thickened.

Use a meat mallet to flatten the veal steaks. Nick the edges to prevent curling.

Press the crumb mixture firmly onto the steaks with your fingers to make it stick.

Cook the steaks in batches until golden brown, then drain on paper towels.

Top with the Parmesan and mozzarella and bake until golden brown.

VEAL PARMIGIANA

Preparation time: 30 minutes
+ chilling
Total cooking time: 30 minutes
Serves 4

4 thin veal steaks
1 cup (100 g/3⅓ oz) dry
    breadcrumbs
½ teaspoon dried basil
¼ cup (25 g/¾ oz) finely grated
    fresh Parmesan
plain flour, for coating
1 egg, lightly beaten
1 tablespoon milk
oilve oil, for frying
1 cup (250 g/8 oz) good-quality
    ready-made tomato pasta sauce
½ cup (50 g/1⅔ oz) finely grated fresh
    Parmesan, extra
100 g (3⅓ oz) mozzarella, thinly sliced

1 Trim the meat of any excess fat and sinew. Place between sheets of plastic wrap and flatten with a meat mallet to 5 mm (¼ inch) thick. Nick the edges to prevent curling. Combine the breadcrumbs, basil and Parmesan on a sheet of greaseproof paper.
2 Coat the veal steaks in flour, shaking off the excess. Working with one at a time, dip the steaks into the combined egg and milk, then coat with the breadcrumb mixture. Lightly shake off the excess. Refrigerate for 30 minutes to firm the coating.
3 Preheat the oven to moderate 180°C (350°F/Gas 4). Heat the oil in a frying pan and brown the veal steaks over medium heat for 2 minutes each side, in batches if necessary. Drain on paper towels.
4 Spread half the pasta sauce into a shallow ovenproof dish. Arrange the veal steaks on top in a single layer and spoon over the remaining sauce.

Top with the Parmesan cheese and mozzarella and bake for 20 minutes, or until the cheeses are melted and golden brown. Serve immediately.

123

PORK WITH MUSTARD AND CREAM SAUCE

Preparation time: 10 minutes
Total cooking time: 25 minutes
Serves 4

2 tablespoons olive oil
4 pork leg steaks

1 onion, sliced into rings
2 cloves garlic, crushed
½ cup (125 ml/4 fl oz) white wine
1 cup (250 ml/8 fl oz) cream
2 tablespoons wholegrain
  mustard
2 tablespoons chopped parsley

1 Heat the oil in a large frying pan; cook the pork for 3–4 minutes each side. Transfer to a plate and set aside.

2 Reduce the heat and add the onion. Cook until soft, then add the garlic and cook for 1 minute further. Add the wine and simmer until the liquid is reduced by half.

3 Stir in the cream and mustard and simmer gently for 5 minutes. Add the pork and simmer for a further 5 minutes. Stir in the parsley and season to taste. Serve immediately, the sauce spooned over the pork.

Fry the pork in oil for 3–4 minutes on each side, until browned.

Cook the onion and garlic until soft and golden, then add the wine and simmer.

Add the pork and then simmer gently for 5 minutes. Stir in the fresh parsley.

LEG OF LAMB WITH PANCETTA STUFFING

Preparation time: 30 minutes
Total cooking time: 1 hour
45 minutes
Serves 6

60 g (2 oz) pancetta, chopped
60 g (2 oz) mild Provolone cheese,
　chopped
2 tablespoons grated Parmesan
⅓ cup (25 g/¾ oz) fresh breadcrumbs
3 tablespoons chopped fresh flat-leaf
　parsley
2 teaspoons chopped fresh rosemary
2 spring onions, chopped
1 egg plus 1 yolk, lightly beaten
1.5 kg (3 lb) boned leg of lamb (ask
　your butcher to do this)
3 tablespoons olive oil
1 onion, chopped
1 carrot, chopped
1 celery stick, chopped
1 cup (250 ml/8 fl oz) dry white wine
1 tablespoon plain flour

1 Preheat the oven to moderately hot 200°C (400°F/Gas 6). Combine the pancetta, cheeses, breadcrumbs, herbs, spring onions and enough beaten egg to form a stuffing that just comes together. Season with pepper.
2 Fill the lamb leg with stuffing, fold over the ends and secure with wooden skewers or string.
3 Heat the oil in a large deep pan and brown the lamb all over. Transfer to a baking dish and sprinkle with salt and pepper. Reheat the pan and add the onion, carrot and celery; toss over the heat for 2 minutes. Add the wine, let the bubbles subside, then pour over the lamb. Bake for 1½ hours, or until tender, turning once or twice.
4 Remove the meat from the dish and leave, loosely covered, for 10 minutes before slicing. Strain the pan juices into a jug and skim off the fat; add water to make up 1½ cups (375 ml/12 fl oz). Heat the flour in a small pan until beginning to brown, remove from the heat and slowly whisk in the pan juices until smooth. Return to the heat and whisk until the sauce boils and thickens. Return the vegetables to the sauce and drizzle over the meat.

Add enough beaten egg to the stuffing mixture to make it just stick together.

Carefully stuff the leg of lamb, pushing the pancetta filling into the cavity.

Skewer together the open ends of the leg of lamb, or tie with string.

Use a large deep pan to brown the lamb as the fat will tend to spit.

125

PROSCIUTTO-WRAPPED PORK WITH POLENTA

Preparation time: 25 minutes
+ 10 minutes resting
Total cooking time: 40 minutes
Serves 4

8 slices prosciutto
4 thin pork fillets (200 g each)
24 large sage leaves
2 tablespoons olive oil
1 cup (250 ml) verjuice or white wine
2 tablespoons balsamic vinegar
200 g cherry tomatoes
20 g butter, melted
1 litre chicken stock
1 cup (170 g) fine instant polenta
50 g butter, extra
100 g mascarpone
½ cup (45 g) grated pecorino cheese

1 Preheat the oven to moderately hot 200°C (400°F/Gas 6). Wrap two slices of prosciutto around each pork fillet, tucking in three sage leaves as you go. Secure with toothpicks.
2 Heat the oil in a frying pan over high heat and cook the pork in batches for 3 minutes, or until golden, then transfer to a baking dish. Deglaze the pan by adding the verjuice and vinegar and scraping up any sediment. Pour the pan juices over the pork, bake for 10 minutes, then cover and rest for 10 minutes. (Leave the oven on.)
3 Lay out the tomatoes in a roasting tin and roast for 10 minutes, or until tender. Keep the tomatoes warm.
4 Meanwhile, brush both sides of the remaining sage leaves with the melted butter, lay on a baking tray and bake for 5 minutes, or until crisp.
5 Bring the stock to the boil in a large saucepan, then slowly add the polenta, stirring constantly. Cook, stirring, for 8–10 minutes, or until smooth and thick. Stir in the butter, mascarpone and pecorino and season.
6 Lay slices of pork on a bed of polenta, drizzle with the cooking juices and top with the tomatoes. Scatter with the sage leaves and serve.

Secure the prosciutto and sage leaves with toothpicks.

Stir the liquid, scraping any sediment from the bottom of the pan.

Roast the tomatoes in a roasting tin until tender.

Cook the polenta, stirring constantly, until smooth and thick.

Trim away any fat from the veal cutlets, then toss them in flour.

Cook the veal cutlets in a single layer until browned on both sides.

Once most of the wine has evaporated, pour in the beef stock and add pepper.

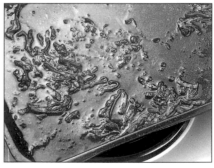

If the pan juices need thickening, simmer them for a while, uncovered.

VEAL CUTLETS WITH SAGE

Preparation time: 25 minutes
Total cooking time: 1 hour
20 minutes
Serves 4–6

8 veal cutlets
2–3 tablespoons plain flour
30 g (1 oz) butter
2 tablespoons olive oil
75 g (2½ oz) sliced ham, cut into strips
½ cup (125 ml/4 fl oz) dry white wine
8 fresh sage leaves, shredded
2 teaspoons chopped fresh rosemary
1 cup (250 ml/8 fl oz) beef stock
freshly ground black pepper

1 Trim any fat from the cutlets then toss in flour. Shake off any excess.
2 Heat the butter and 1 tablespoon of the oil in a large baking dish. When foaming, add the veal cutlets in a single layer and cook until browned on both sides. Drain on paper towels. Wipe the pan clean, then add the remaining oil and the ham; toss over the heat for a few minutes.
3 Return the cutlets to the pan, then pour in the wine with the herbs. Simmer, uncovered, until most of the liquid has evaporated. Add the stock and black pepper. Bring back to the boil, reduce the heat and simmer, covered (with foil if necessary), for about 1 hour, or until the cutlets are tender, turning once during cooking.
4 Transfer the cutlets to a serving dish and keep warm. If the pan juices are very thin, simmer uncovered until thickened. Season with salt to taste, if necessary, then pour over the cutlets. Garnish with fresh sage.

127

BEEF OLIVES WITH ARTICHOKE STUFFING

Preparation time: 20 minutes
Total cooking time: 50 minutes
Serves 4

8 slices beef topside (about
   80 g/2⅔ oz each slice)
100 g (3⅓ oz) prosciutto, finely
   chopped
50 g (1⅔ oz) butter, melted
4 artichoke hearts
2 tablespoons chopped fresh thyme
plain flour, for coating
⅓ cup (80 ml/2¾ fl oz) dry white wine
½ cup (125 ml/4 fl oz) beef stock

1 Flatten each beef slice with a meat mallet (or rolling pin) until wafer thin. Mix together the prosciutto and 1 tablespoon of the butter and spread over the beef slices. Roughly chop each artichoke into quarters and arrange the pieces evenly over the prosciutto. Sprinkle with thyme and salt and pepper to taste.
2 Roll up the beef slices around the stuffing. Tie each beef olive with string to hold it together.
3 Heat the remaining butter in a frying pan. Roll the beef olives in a little flour, shake off the excess and fry until browned. Add the wine and the beef stock, then cover and cook for 45 minutes, or until tender. Turn the meat several times during cooking.
4 Remove the beef olives with a slotted spoon, cover and keep warm. Return the pan to the heat and reduce the sauce until slightly thickened, if necessary. Season to taste with salt and black pepper. Remove the string from the beef olives and pour the sauce over before serving.

COOK'S FILE

Note: To make beef stock at home, bake 2 kg (4 lb) beef bones at 210°C (415°F/Gas 6–7) for 30 minutes, then simmer in a large pan with chopped carrots, onions, celery, bouquet garni and 3 litres water for 4 hours. Ready-made stock in a tetra pack is very convenient but can be salty—try using half stock, half water.

Cover the beef with a sheet of plastic wrap and flatten with a meat mallet.

Roll the beef around the filling and then secure with string.

Add the wine, a little more salt and black pepper and the beef stock.

Remove the beef olives from the pan, then reduce the sauce to thicken.

CHICKEN MARSALA

Preparation time: 10 minutes
Total cooking time: 25 minutes
Serves 4

4 chicken breast fillets
2 tablespoons oil
60 g (2 oz) butter
1 clove garlic, crushed
2 cups (500 ml/16 fl oz) chicken
  stock
⅓ cup (80 ml/2¾ fl oz) Marsala
2 teaspoons plain flour
3 tablespoons cream
2 teaspoons Worcestershire sauce

1 Trim the chicken of excess fat and sinew. Heat the oil in a heavy-based frying pan and add the chicken. Cook over medium heat for 4 minutes on each side, or until cooked through and lightly golden. Remove the chicken, cover loosely with foil and keep warm. Drain off any fat from the pan.
2 Add the butter and garlic to the pan and stir over medium heat for 2 minutes. Add the combined stock and Marsala and bring to the boil. Reduce the heat and simmer for 10 minutes, or until the liquid has reduced by half.
3 Blend together the flour, cream and Worcestershire sauce; add a little of the hot liquid and blend to a paste.

Add this to the pan and then stir over medium heat until the sauce boils and thickens. Season with salt and black pepper and then pour over the chicken fillets. Delicious with pasta.

COOK'S FILE
Variation: Marsala is a sweet wine and so makes a sweet-tasting sauce. Port or any dry red wine can be used instead. Boiling wine evaporates the alcohol, leaving the flavour but not the intoxicating qualities. Chicken thighs or drumsticks can be used instead of breast fillets.
Hint: Blending the flour to a paste first prevents lumps forming when it is added to the sauce.

Cook the chicken in a frying pan until lightly golden on each side.

Mix together the stock and Marsala, then add to the pan and bring to the boil.

Add the flour, cream and Worcestershire sauce and stir over heat until thickened.

CHICKEN CACCIATORE

Preparation time: 20 minutes
Total cooking time: 1 hour
Serves 6

3 tablespoons olive oil
12 small chicken drumsticks
1 large onion, finely chopped
3 cloves garlic, crushed
440 g (14 oz) can crushed tomatoes
½ cup (90 g/3 oz) black olives

1 cup (250 ml/8 fl oz) tomato purée
½ cup (125 ml/4 fl oz) white wine
½ cup (125 ml/4 fl oz) chicken stock
125 g (4 oz) button mushrooms, quartered
1 tablespoon chopped fresh oregano
2 teaspoons chopped fresh thyme
2 teaspoons soft brown sugar

1 Heat half the oil in a large heavy-based pan and brown the drumsticks in small batches over high heat.
2 Heat the remaining oil in a frying pan and cook the onion and garlic for 10 minutes, or until golden. Remove from the pan and add to the chicken.
3 Add the remaining ingredients to the frying pan. Bring to the boil, reduce the heat and then simmer for 10 minutes. Season to taste with salt and pepper. Pour over the chicken, stir to combine, cover and simmer for 35 minutes, or until very tender.

COOK'S FILE
Storage time: Can be made up to 2 days ahead.

Cut the mushrooms into quarters and finely chop the onion.

Cook the drumsticks in batches so they brown—if overcrowded they will stew.

Simmer the tomato mixture, then pour over the chicken and mix together.

LAMB SHANKS WITH LENTILS

Preparation time: 20 minutes
Total cooking time: 2 hours
Serves 2

1 cup (250 g/8 oz) red lentils, rinsed and drained
½ teaspoon salt
2 celery sticks, diced
1 green capsicum, diced
2 cloves garlic, finely chopped
2 onions, finely chopped

4 small lamb shanks
800 g (1 lb 10 oz) can crushed tomatoes
3 bay leaves
3 teaspoons chopped fresh marjoram
3 teaspoons chopped thyme

1 Preheat the oven to moderate 180°C (350°F/Gas 4). Spread the lentils in the base of a large ovenproof casserole dish and sprinkle with salt.
2 Add the celery, capsicum, garlic and onion. Layer the lamb shanks over the top, then pour over the tomatoes. Add the bay leaves, fresh marjoram and thyme. Cover the dish (with foil if you don't have a lid) and bake for 2 hours.
3 Skim off any fat which may have formed on the surface. Remove the bay leaves and stir together the lentils, meat and vegetables before serving.

COOK'S FILE
Note: Red lentils are smaller and softer than green or brown lentils and so do not need to be soaked before cooking.
Variation: Lamb shanks are a very economical cut of meat—use chump chops if shanks are not available.

Spread the lentils in a large dish and sprinkle with salt.

Place the vegetables over the lentils, layer the lamb on top and add the tomatoes.

Remove the bay leaves and give the dish a quick stir before serving.

Chicken Cacciatore (top) and Lamb Shanks with Lentils

ROAST GARLIC CHICKEN WITH VEGETABLES

Preparation time: 20 minutes
Total cooking time: 1 hour
20 minutes
Serves 4

315 g (10 oz) orange sweet
   potatoes, peeled and cut into
   wedges
315 g (10 oz) pontiac potatoes,
   peeled and cut into wedges

315 g (10 oz) pumpkin, peeled and
   cut into wedges
1 chicken, cut into 8 pieces, or 1.5 kg
   (3 lb) chicken pieces
3 tablespoons olive oil
1 tablespoon fresh thyme leaves
20 large garlic cloves, unpeeled (see
   Note)
½ teaspoon sea salt

1 Preheat the oven to hot 220°C
(425°F/Gas 7). Bring a large pan of
salted water to the boil and cook the
sweet potatoes, pontiac potatoes and
pumpkin for 5 minutes. Drain well.

2 Put the chicken and vegetables in
a baking dish, drizzle with olive oil
and scatter with thyme leaves and
garlic cloves. Sprinkle with the sea salt.
3 Roast for 1 hour 15 minutes,
turning every 20 minutes or so, until
the chicken, potatoes and pumpkin
become well browned and crisp at
the edges. Serve immediately.

COOK'S FILE
Note: This seems a lot of garlic, but it
becomes sweet and mild when cooked.
Squeeze the roasted flesh from the
garlic onto the chicken and vegetables.

*Boil the sweet and pontiac potatoes and
pumpkin for 5 minutes, then drain.*

*Drizzle the chicken and vegetables with
oil then sprinkle with garlic and thyme.*

*Turn the chicken and vegetables every
20 minutes, until browned and crisp.*

OSSO BUCCO

Preparation time: 30 minutes
Total cooking time: 2 hours
50 minutes
Serves 4–6

2 tablespoons plain flour
freshly ground black pepper
4 veal shanks (osso bucco), cut into
　　short lengths
2 tablespoons oil
2 cloves garlic, crushed
1 large onion, chopped
1 large carrot, chopped
⅔ cup (170 ml/5½ fl oz) dry white
　　wine
⅔ cup (170 ml/5½ fl oz) beef stock
425 g (13½oz) can tomatoes
3 tablespoons tomato paste
½ teaspoon caster sugar

GREMOLATA
⅓ cup (7 g/¼ oz) fresh parsley
1 clove garlic, crushed
2 teaspoons grated lemon rind

1 Preheat the oven to moderate
180°C (350°F/Gas 4). Lightly grease
a 12-cup (3-litre) baking dish.
Combine the flour and pepper on a
sheet of greaseproof paper and
lightly coat the osso bucco. Shake
off the excess.
2 Heat the oil in a heavy-based pan.
Brown the meat on both sides over
medium-high heat; drain on paper
towels. Transfer to the baking dish.
3 Add the garlic and onion to the
pan and cook, stirring, until just
soft. Add the carrot, wine, stock,
crushed tomatoes, tomato paste and
sugar. Bring to the boil, reduce the
heat and simmer for 5 minutes.
Spoon over the meat, cover with foil
and bake for 2 hours. Uncover and
bake for a further 30 minutes, or
until tender.
4 To make Gremolata: Finely chop
the parsley, then mix with the garlic
and rind. Just before serving, sprinkle
Gremolata over Osso Bucco.

COOK'S FILE
Storage time: Cook Osso Bucco up to
1 day ahead and keep, covered, in the
refrigerator, or freeze for 1 month. Make
Gremolata just before serving.

Put the flour and pepper on greaseproof paper and lightly coat the osso bucco.

Brown the meat in batches—if the pan is overcrowded it will stew rather than fry.

Spoon the tomato mixture over the meat, cover with foil and bake until tender.

Finely chop the parsley and mix together with the garlic and lemon rind.

PESTO LAMB CUTLETS

Preparation time: 40 minutes
+ chilling
Total cooking time: 20 minutes
Serves 4

12 lamb cutlets
1 egg
3 tablespoons pesto
1 teaspoon wholegrain mustard

2 tablespoons cornflour
1 cup (80 g/2⅔ oz) fresh
  breadcrumbs
⅓ cup (35 g/1¼ oz) grated Parmesan
⅓ cup (50 g/1⅔ oz) pine nuts, finely
  chopped

1 Trim any fat from the cutlets and
scrape the flesh from the bone to give
them a nice shape. Whisk together
the egg, pesto, mustard and cornflour.
2 Mix the breadcrumbs, Parmesan
and pine nuts in a bowl. Dip each

cutlet into the pesto then breadcrumb
mixtures. Chill for 30 minutes.
3 Shallow-fry the cutlets in oil, in
batches, for 5 minutes each side.

COOK'S FILE
Note: To make pesto, process 2
bunches basil leaves, 4 tablespoons
toasted pine nuts, 2 crushed cloves
garlic and 4 tablespoons grated
Parmesan until well blended. Still
processing, slowly add 4 tablespoons
olive oil in a stream, until well mixed.

*Whisk together the egg, pesto, mustard
and cornflour.*

*Dip the cutlets in the pesto mixture, then
the breadcrumb mixture.*

*Turn the cutlets with a spatula, taking
care not to dislodge the crumb coating.*

ITALIAN SAUSAGE CASSEROLE

Preparation time: 15 minutes
Total cooking time: 45 minutes
Serves 4

2 large red capsicums
1 tablespoon olive oil
2 large red onions, sliced into thick
    wedges
2 cloves garlic, finely chopped
600 g Italian-style thin pork sausages
300 g can chickpeas, drained
150 g flat mushrooms, thickly sliced
½ cup (125 ml) dry white wine
2 bay leaves
2 teaspoons chopped fresh rosemary
400 g can diced tomatoes

1 Cut the capsicums into large pieces, removing the seeds and membrane. Place skin-side-up, under a hot grill until the skin blackens and blisters. Allow to cool in a plastic bag. Peel away the skin, and slice diagonally into thick strips.
2 Meanwhile, heat the oil in a large non-stick frying pan. Add the onion and garlic, and stir over medium heat for 6 minutes, or until the onion is soft and browned. Remove the onion from the pan and set aside. Add the sausages to the same pan. Cook over medium heat, turning occasionally, for 8 minutes, or until the sausages are browned. Remove the sausages and slice them diagonally into 3 cm pieces.
3 Combine the capsicum, onion, sausage, chickpeas and mushrooms

in the pan and cook over medium–high heat.
4 Add the wine, bay leaves and rosemary. Bring to the boil, then reduce the heat to low and simmer for 3 minutes. Stir in the tomatoes and simmer for 20 minutes, or until the sauce has thickened slightly. Remove the bay leaves and season to taste with sugar, salt and cracked black pepper. Delicious served with fettucine, noodles, grilled ciabatta bread, mashed potato, soft polenta, or Parmesan shavings.

COOK'S FILE
Storage time: This casserole can be stored in the refrigerator for up to 2 days.

Grill the capsicums under a hot grill until the skin blackens and blisters.

Remove the skin from the cooled capsicums and slice them into thin strips.

Use a pair of tongs to hold the sausages as you slice them into 3 cm pieces.

BEEF POT ROAST WITH EGGPLANT AND SWEET POTATO

Preparation time: 20 minutes
Cooking time: 1 hour 15 minutes
Serves 4

1 x 1 kg piece topside beef
2 tablespoons oil
1 cup beefstock
1 medium onion, sliced
1 clove garlic, crushed
4 large tomatoes, peeled,
    seeded,chopped
1 teaspoon ground cumin
1 teaspoon turmeric
1 teaspoon finely grated lemon rind
2 tablespoons lemon juice
1 medium eggplant, cut into 3 cm
cubes
1 medium sweet potato, halved,
    cut into 1 cm slices
2 tablespoons plain flour
3 tablespoons water
1 tablespoon chopped fresh
    coriander

1 Trim meat of any excess fat and sinew. Heat oil in a deep, heavy-based pan, add whole piece of meat, cook over a medium-high heat until well brownedon all sides.
2 Remove pan from heat, add stock, onion, garlic, tomato, cumin turmeric, lemon rind and juice. Reduce heat to low, return pan to heat. Cover, bring to simmering point, simmer for 45 minutes.
3 Add eggplant and sweet potato,

cook for 30 minutes, uncovered, until meat and vegetables are tender. Remove meat from the sauce. Leave in a warm place, covered with foil, 10 minutes before slicing. Combine flour and water to make a smooth paste. Add to sauce with coriander, stir over medium heat until sauce boils and thickens, cook 3 minutes. Pour over sliced meat to serve.

COOK'S FILE
Storage time: Cook this dish just before serving.
Hint: Never allow a pot roast to boil. Long, slow cooking keeps the meat tender and moist.

LAMB CASSEROLE WITH BEANS

Preparation time: 25 minutes
+ overnight soaking
Total cooking time: 2 hours
15 minutes
Serves 6

1½ cups (300 g) borlotti beans or red
  kidney beans
1 kg boned leg lamb
1½ tablespoons olive oil
2 rashers bacon, rind removed,
  chopped
1 large onion, chopped
2 cloves garlic, crushed

1 large carrot, chopped
2 cups (500 ml) dry red wine
1 tablespoon tomato paste
1½ cups (375 ml) beef stock
2 large sprigs fresh rosemary
2 sprigs fresh thyme

1 Put the beans in a bowl and cover with plenty of water. Leave to soak overnight, then drain well.
2 Preheat the oven to warm 160°C (315°F/Gas 2–3). Trim any excess fat from lamb and cut into 3 cm pieces.
3 Heat 1 tablespoon oil in a large flameproof casserole. Add half the meat and toss over medium–high heat for 2 minutes, or until browned. Remove from pan and repeat with remaining lamb. Remove from pan.

4 Heat the remaining olive oil in the casserole and add the bacon and onion. Cook over medium heat for 3 minutes, or until the onion is translucent. Add the garlic and carrot, and cook for 1 minute, or until aromatic.
5 Return the meat and any juices to the pan, increase the heat to high and add the wine. Bring to the boil and cook for 2 minutes. Add the beans, tomato paste, stock, rosemary and thyme, bring to the boil, then cover and cook in the oven for 2 hours, or until the meat is tender. Stir occasionally during cooking. Skim off any excess fat, remove the sprigs of herbs and season. Serve with bread.

Remove any excess fat from the lamb then cut it into 3 cm pieces.

Heat the oil then add the lamb and toss until browned all over.

Return the meat and juices to the pan, add the wine, and bring to the boil.

SLOW-COOKED SHANKS

Preparation time: 20 minutes
Total cooking time: 3 hours
Serves 4

2 tablespoons oil
4 lamb shanks
2 red onions, sliced
10 cloves garlic, peeled
400 g can chopped tomatoes

½ cup (125 ml) dry white wine
1 bay leaf
1 teaspoon grated lemon rind
1 large red capsicum, chopped
3 tablespoons chopped fresh parsley

1 Preheat the oven to warm 170°C (325°F/Gas 3). Heat the oil in a large flameproof casserole dish, add the shanks in batches and cook over high heat until browned on all sides.
2 Add the onion and garlic, and cook until softened, then add the

tomato, wine, bay leaf, lemon rind, capsicum and ½ cup (125 ml) water and bring to the boil. Cover and cook in the oven for 2–2½ hours, or until the meat is tender and falling off the bone and the sauce is thickened. Season to taste with salt and cracked black pepper.
3 Sprinkle the parsley over the top and serve with couscous or polenta.

Heat the oil in a pan and brown the shanks in batches.

Add the onion and garlic to the pan and cook until softened

Add the tomato, wine, bay leaf, lemon rind, capsicum and water.

BABY CHICKENS IN RED WINE

Preparation time: 25 minutes
Total cooking time: 1 hour
5 minutes
Serves 4

2 x 400 g baby chickens
plain flour
¼ cup olive oil
16 baby onions
125 g bacon pieces, chopped
2 cloves garlic, crushed

3 cups red wine
½ cup brandy or cognac
4 bay leaves
1 tablespoon chopped fresh thyme
250 g button mushrooms
salt and freshly ground black pepper

1 Remove giblets and any large deposits of fat from the chickens. Wipe and pat dry with paper towels. Using poultry shears cut chickens into quarters. Toss lightly in flour; shake off excess.
2 Heat oil in large heavy-based pan; add chicken. Cook for 2 minutes on each side or until lightly browned.

Add onions, bacon, garlic, wine, brandy, bay leaves and thyme. Bring to boil, reduce heat. Cook, covered for 30 minutes, stirring occasionally.
3 Add mushrooms; continue cooking for 30 minutes more or until chickens are tender. Remove lid for last 15 minutes to thicken sauce. Season to taste. Serve hot.

COOK'S FILE
Storage time: Can be made up to 2 days ahead and store covered in the refrigerator. Reheat just before serving.
Hint: Any robust red wine (burgundy or claret) is ideal for use in this recipe.

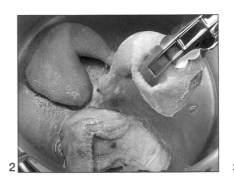

FLORENTINE CHICKEN WITH ROAST CAPSICUM

Preparation time: 35 minutes
Total cooking time: 45 minutes
Serves 4

4 (1.7 kg) chicken maryland pieces
12 English spinach leaves
250 g ricotta cheese
½ cup grated Parmesan cheese
3 cloves garlic, crushed
1 medium onion, thinly sliced
salt and freshly ground pepper
60 g butter or margarine, melted
2 large red capsicums, halved,
seeds removed

1 Preheat oven to moderate 180°C. Trim chicken of any excess fat and sinew.

Gently ease the skin away from the chicken meat, leaving skin attached on one side and forming a pocket.
2 Remove stalks from spinach. Add leaves to a medium pan of simmering water. Cover and cook for 2 inutes or until tender. Remove from heat; drain and squeeze out excess liquid. Chop spinach finely.
3 In a medium bowl, combine the spinach with ricotta, Parmesan cheese and garlic. Spoon mixture carefully between skin and flesh of chicken. Use toothpicks to secure opening. Place chicken in shallow baking dish. Top with onion rings, salt and black pepper; drizzle with melted butter. Bake 45 minutes or until golden and cooked through.
4 Place capsicum cut-side down on a baking sheet. Bake 30 minutes (in same oven with chicken) or until skin

lifts away from flesh. Peel skin off peppers, slice and serve with chicken.

COOK'S FILE
Storage time: This can be assembled a day ahead. Store, covered with plastic wrap, in the refrigerator. Bake just before serving. The capsicum can be roasted a day ahead and refrigerated. Reheat the peppers in the oven while the chicken is cooking.

ROAST LEG OF LAMB WITH LEEK AND PARSLEY SEASONING

Preparation time: 10 minutes
Cooking time: 1 hour to 1 hour 45 minutes
Serves 6

1 x 1.8 kg leg of lamb, tunnel boned
30 g butter
1 large leek, white part only, finely chopped
2 cloves garlic, crushed
1 cup roughly chopped fresh parsley
½ cup cream
1½ cups chicken stock

1 Preheat oven to moderate 180°C. Trim meat of excess fat and sinew. Heat butter in pan, add leek and garlic, stir over medium heat until soft. Add the parsley and cream. Cook, stirring occasionally, for 5 minutes or until the liquid has evaporated. Leave to cool.
2 Spoon the mixture into the meat. Tuck in the ends of meat to enclose mixture, tie meat securely with string to retain its shape during cooking. Place in deep baking dish, add stock.
3 Roast meat for 1 hour for a rare result, 1 hour 15 minutes for medium and 1 hour 45 minutes for well done. Baste the meat

occasionally with pan juices. Remove from oven. Leave in a warm place for 10 minutes, covered with foil. Remove string before slicing. Strain pan juices into a jug, serve with the sliced meat.

COOK'S NOTES
Storage time: Cook this dish just before serving. Hint: Ask your butcher to tunnel bone the leg of lamb for you; tunnel boning ensures that the stuffing is securely enclosed during cooking. Meat is easier to slice if it is left a few minutes in a warm place after cooking.

1

2

3

BAKED CHICKEN ROLLS

Preparation time: 35 minutes
Total cooking time: 40 minutes
Serves 4

8 chicken thigh fillets
125 g sun-dried tomatoes
½ cup grated cheddar cheese
⅓ cup firmly packed fresh basil
  leaves
8 slices prosciutto or thin-sliced ham

WARM MUSTARD DRESSING
½ cup cream
2 teaspoons balsamic vinegar

2 cloves garlic, crushed
3 teaspoons mustard

1 Preheat oven to moderate 180°C.
Remove excess fat and sinew from
chicken. Lay chicken thighs out,
smooth-side down, on work surface.
Place a sheet of plastic wrap over
chicken and flatten lightly using a
meat mallet or rolling pin. Set aside.
2 In food processor bowl, combine
sun-dried tomatoes, cheese and basil.
Process just until finely chopped.
3 Spoon the tomato mixture onto
the end of each thigh and roll to
enclose. Wrap each roll firmly in a
slice of prosciutto. Place rolls into a
shallow baking dish. Bake for 20–30

minutes or until cooked through.
Slice chicken and serve with Warm
Mustard Dressing.
4 To make Warm Mustard Dressing:
Combine all ingredients in a small
pan. Stir over medium heat, until hot.

COOK'S FILE
Storage time: You can assemble the
rolls up to 2 hours ahead and store in
the fridge. Cook just before serving..

ROAST LAMB WITH ASPARAGUS AND PARMESAN FILLING

Preparation time: 20 minutes
Cooking time: 50 minutes to
1 hour 10 minutes
Serves 4

1 x 2 kg boned shoulder of lamb
30g butter
2 tablespoons oil
½ cup white wine
½ cup chicken stock

ASPARAGUS AND PARMESAN FILLING
100g asparagus spears, cut into
 1 cm pieces
15 g butter
1 small onion, finely chopped
3 slices prosciutto, finely chopped
½ cup/about 30 g fresh white
 breadcrumbs
3 tablespoons freshly grated
 Parmesan cheese
1 egg, lightly beaten

1 Preheat to moderate 180°C. Trim meat of any excess fat and sinew. To make the Asparagus and Parmesan Filling: Cook asparagus in boiling water for 3 minutes or until tender. Drain, rinse under cold water. Heat butter in pan, add onion, stir over a low heat until soft. Add prosciutto,stir until brown; remove from heat. Add the breadcrumbs, cheese, egg and asparagus; stir until combined.
2 Open meat out flat, fat side down. Press Filling over meat. Roll up firmly, tucking in edges; tie meat securely with string at regular intervals to retain its shape.

3 Heat butter and oil in deep baking dish on top of stove; add meat, brown meat all over on high heat. Add wine and stock,transfer dish to oven. Roast meat 50 minutes for rare result, 1 hour for medium result and 1 hour 10 minutes for well done. Baste meat occasionally with pan juices. Remove from oven. Leave in a warm place for

10 minutes, covered with foil. Remove string before slicing. Strain pan juices, pour over meat to serve

COOK'S FILE
Storage time: Cook just before serving. Leftovers can be stored, covered, in the fridge for 2 days. Store meat and filling separately.
Hint: Do not use canned asparagus.

VEGETABLES AND SALADS

EGGPLANT PARMIGIANA

Preparation time: 30 minutes
Total cooking time: 1 hour
15 minutes
Serves 6–8

3 tablespoons olive oil
1 onion, diced
2 cloves garlic, crushed
1.25 kg (2 lb 8 oz) tomatoes, peeled
    and chopped
1 kg (2 lb) eggplants
250 g (8 oz) bocconcini, sliced
185 g (6 oz) Cheddar, finely grated
1 cup (50 g/1⅔ oz) basil leaves
½ cup (50 g/1⅔ oz) grated Parmesan

1 Heat the oil in a frying pan; add the onion and cook over moderate heat until soft. Add the garlic and cook for 1 minute. Add the tomato and simmer for 15 minutes. Season with salt to taste. Preheat the oven to moderately hot 200°C (400°F/Gas 6).
2 Slice the eggplants very thinly and shallow-fry in oil in batches for 3–4 minutes, or until golden brown. Drain on paper towels.
3 Place one third of the eggplant in a 7-cup (1.75 litre) ovenproof dish. Top with half the bocconcini and Cheddar. Repeat the layers, finishing with a layer of eggplant.
4 Pour over the tomato mixture. Scatter with torn basil leaves, then Parmesan. Bake for 40 minutes.

Fry the onion and garlic in the oil, then add the chopped tomato.

Shallow-fry the eggplant in batches, then drain on paper towels.

Arrange layers of eggplant, bocconcini and Cheddar in the dish.

Pour over the tomato sauce and sprinkle with torn basil leaves and Parmesan.

STUFFED ZUCCHINI

Preparation time: 20 minutes
Total cooking time: 45 minutes
Serves 4

8 zucchini
35 g (1¼ oz) white bread, crusts
    removed
milk, for soaking
125 g (4 oz) ricotta cheese
3 tablespoons grated Cheddar

⅓ cup (35 g/1¼ oz) grated Parmesan
2 teaspoons chopped fresh oregano
2 teaspoons chopped fresh thyme
1 clove garlic, crushed
1 egg yolk

1 Preheat the oven to moderately hot 190°C (375°F/Gas 5). Cook the zucchini in boiling salted water for 5 minutes, then drain. Meanwhile, soak the bread in milk until soft, then squeeze dry. Cut the zucchini in half and scoop out the flesh with a teaspoon.

2 Chop the zucchini flesh finely. Place in a bowl and add the bread, cheeses, herbs, garlic, egg yolk and season with salt and pepper. Mix together, adding a little milk to make it bind together if necessary.
3 Fill the zucchini shells with the stuffing. Brush an ovenproof baking dish with oil and arrange the zucchini close together. Bake in the oven for 35–40 minutes, until golden on top. Serve immediately.

Cut the zucchini in half and scoop out the flesh with a teaspoon.

Combine the zucchini, cheeses, herbs, garlic and egg yolk in a bowl.

Arrange the stuffed zucchini close together in the oiled baking dish.

146

Cook the leek until soft, then add the stock, thyme and potato.

Lift out half the potato with tongs and put into an ovenproof dish.

Spoon the leek and stock mixture around the side, trying to keep the top dry.

Bake, uncovered, until the potatoes on top are golden brown.

OVEN-BAKED POTATO, LEEK AND OLIVES

Preparation time: 20 minutes
Total cooking time: 1 hour
Serves 4–6

2 tablespoons extra virgin olive oil
1 leek, finely sliced
1½ cups (375 ml/12 fl oz) chicken stock
2 teaspoons chopped fresh thyme
1 kg (2 lb) potatoes, unpeeled, cut into thin slices
6–8 pitted black olives, sliced
½ cup (50 g/1⅔ oz) freshly grated Parmesan
30 g (1 oz) butter, chopped

1 Preheat the oven to moderate 180°C (350°F/Gas 4). Brush a shallow 5-cup (1.25 litre) ovenproof dish with olive oil. Heat remaining oil in a large pan and cook the leek over moderate heat until soft. Add the stock, thyme and potato. Cover and leave to simmer for 5 minutes.
2 Using tongs, lift out half the potato and put in the ovenproof dish. Sprinkle with olives and Parmesan and season with salt and pepper.
3 Layer with the remaining potato, then spoon the leek and stock mixture in at the side of the dish, keeping the top dry.
4 Scatter chopped butter over the potato and then bake, uncovered, for 50 minutes, or until cooked and golden brown. Leave in a warm place for about 10 minutes before serving.

COOK'S FILE
Note: Keeping the top layer of potato dry as you pour in the stock mixture will give it a crisp finish.

BEAN AND CAPSICUM STEW

Preparation time: 20 minutes
+ overnight soaking
Total cooking time: 1 hour
35 minutes
Serves 4–6

1 cup (200 g) dried haricot beans
  (see Note)
2 tablespoons olive oil
2 large cloves garlic, crushed
1 red onion, halved and cut into thin
  wedges
1 red capsicum, cut into 1.5 cm
  cubes
1 green capsicum, cut into
  1.5 cm cubes
2 x 400 g cans chopped tomatoes
2 tablespoons tomato paste
2 cups (500 ml) vegetable stock
2 tablespoons chopped fresh basil
⅔ cup (125 g) Kalamata olives, pitted
1–2 teaspoons soft brown sugar

1 Put the beans in a large bowl,
cover with cold water and soak
overnight. Rinse well, then transfer
to a saucepan, cover with cold water
and cook for 45 minutes, or until
just tender. Drain.
2 Heat the oil in a large saucepan.
Cook the garlic and onion over
medium heat for 2–3 minutes, or
until the onion is soft. Add the red
and green capsicums and cook for a
further 5 minutes.
3 Stir in the tomato, tomato paste,
stock and beans. Simmer, covered,

for 40 minutes, or until the beans are
cooked through. Stir in the basil,
olives and sugar. Season with salt and
pepper. Serve hot with crusty bread.

COOK'S FILE
Note: 1 cup of dried haricot beans
yields about 2½ cups cooked beans.
You can use 2½ cups tinned haricot or
borlotti beans instead if you prefer.

*Cook the garlic, onion and capsicum in
a large saucepan.*

*Simmer the mixture for 40 minutes, or
until the beans are cooked through.*

PEPPERONATA TART

Preparation time: 30 minutes
+ chilling
Total cooking time: 1 hour
Serves 4–6

2½ cups (310 g/9¾ oz) plain flour
pinch of cayenne pepper
125 g (4 oz) butter, cubed
90 g (3 oz) cream cheese, cubed
1 egg yolk, beaten
1 tablespoon lemon juice

FILLING
1 large red capsicum
1 large green capsicum
2 large yellow capsicums
2 tablespoons olive oil
3 large onions, sliced into rings
400 g (12⅔ oz) can chopped
    tomatoes
fresh thyme leaves, to garnish

1 Sift flour, a pinch of salt and
cayenne into a food processor. Add
butter, cream cheese, combined egg
yolk and lemon juice and process in
short bursts, adding 2–3 tablespoons
water, until mix forms a firm dough
when pressed together. Turn onto a
lightly floured surface and gather
into a ball. Wrap in plastic wrap and
chill for 30 minutes. Roll out to fit a
25 cm (10 inch) greased springform
tin, to cover the base and halfway up
the side. Refrigerate for 30 minutes.
2 Preheat oven to moderately hot
200°C (400°F/Gas 6). Put baking
paper over pastry and fill with rice or
dried beans. Bake for 15 minutes,
then reduce oven to moderate 180°C
(350°F/Gas 4), remove the beans and
paper and cook for 15–20 minutes,
or until golden brown. Cool.
3 To make Filling: Cut capsicums
into large pieces and de-seed. Place,
skin-side-up, under a hot grill until
black. Cool under a tea towel.
Remove the skins and chop the flesh.
4 Heat the oil and fry the onions for
3–4 minutes, or until soft. Add the
tomatoes, capsicum and seasoning.
Cook, uncovered, over low heat for
10 minutes until liquid has reduced.
Cool, then spoon into the pastry case
and sprinkle with thyme to serve.

*Process until the mixture forms a firm
dough when pressed together.*

*Cooling the capsicum under a tea towel
makes the skin easier to peel away.*

*Use uncooked rice, chickpeas or beans
for blind baking pastry.*

*Spoon the capsicum and tomato filling
into the pastry base.*

BAKED MUSHROOMS

Preparation time: 15 minutes
Total cooking time: 15 minutes
Serves 4

250 g (8 oz) button mushrooms
200 g (6½ oz) oyster mushrooms
200 g (6½ oz) shiitake mushrooms
100 g (3⅓ oz) Swiss brown
 mushrooms

TOPPING
1 cup (80 g/2⅔ oz) fresh
 breadcrumbs

¼ cup (25 g/¾ oz) freshly grated
 Parmesan
2 tablespoons chopped fresh flat-leaf
 parsley
1 tablespoon chopped fresh thyme
2 cloves garlic, crushed
1 teaspoon cracked pepper
2 tablespoons extra virgin olive oil

1 Preheat the oven to moderate
180°C (350°F/Gas 4). Wipe the
mushrooms with damp paper towel.
Trim away the hard tips and discard.
Cut any large mushrooms in half
lengthways.
2 Sprinkle the base of a large baking
dish with a little water. Place the

mushrooms in a single layer in the
dish, stems upwards.
3 To make Topping: Mix together
the breadcrumbs, Parmesan, herbs,
garlic and pepper, sprinkle over the
mushrooms and drizzle with oil. Bake
for 12–15 minutes and serve warm.

COOK'S FILE
Note: Use day-old bread which is
slightly stale to make breadcrumbs.
Simply remove the crusts and chop in
a food processor until crumbs form.
Hint: Always wipe mushrooms clean
with a damp paper towel—washing will
make them soggy.

*Trim the hard tips from the stalks and
cut any large mushrooms in half.*

*Place the mushrooms, stems upwards, in
one layer in a baking dish.*

*Mix together the breadcrumbs, cheese,
herbs, garlic and pepper.*

ROLLED CAPSICUMS

Preparation time: 20 minutes
+ 30 minutes marinating
Total cooking time: 10 minutes
Serves 6

2 large red capsicums
2 large yellow capsicums
2 large green capsicums
3 tablespoons olive oil
1 teaspoon lemon juice

2 cloves garlic, crushed
185 g (6 oz) flaked tuna, drained
100 g (3⅓ oz) anchovies, drained and
  chopped
⅓ cup (60 g/2 oz) black olives, pitted
  and chopped
2 tablespoons capers, drained
1 tablespoon chopped fresh parsley

1 Cut the capsicums into quarters lengthways, remove the seeds and membrane and brush skin with a little oil. Cook until a hot grill, skin-side-up, until the skins are black and blistered. Cover with a tea towel and leave to cool. Peel away the skin.
2 Combine the remaining oil, lemon juice, garlic and a little salt. Marinate the capsicums in this for 30 minutes. In another bowl, mix together the tuna, anchovies, olives and capers.
3 Drain the capsicums, reserving the marinade, and place 2 teaspoons of tuna filling on each piece. Roll up and arrange on a serving dish. Drizzle with the reserved marinade and then garnish with chopped parsley and cracked black pepper.

Remove the seeds and membrane from the capsicums.

Leave the capsicum in the marinade for 30 minutes.

Place 2 teaspoonsful of filling on each piece of capsicum and roll up.

CAPONATA

Preparation time: 25 minutes
Total cooking time: 35 minutes
Serves 6

3 tablespoons olive oil
2 onions, sliced
2 red capsicums, thinly sliced
4 cloves garlic, finely chopped
4 celery sticks, sliced
1 large eggplant (500 g/1 lb), cubed
1 kg (2.2 lb) fresh tomatoes, peeled
    and chopped

2 tablespoons fresh thyme
    leaves
2 tablespoons sugar
½ cup (125 ml/4 fl oz) red wine
    vinegar
125 g (4 oz) pitted green olives,
    rinsed well and drained
2 tablespoons capers,
    drained

1 Heat the oil in a large frying pan and add the onion, capsicum, garlic, celery and eggplant. Cover and then leave to simmer over low heat for 20 minutes. Season to taste with salt and freshly ground black pepper.

2 Add tomatoes and thyme; leave to simmer, uncovered, for 15 minutes.
3 Add the sugar, vinegar, olives and capers to the vegetables and mix well. Taste and season again if necessary before serving. Serve warm or at room temperature.

COOK'S FILE
Hint: Peel fresh tomatoes by scoring a cross in the top of the tomato and placing in a bowl of boiling water for 1 minute. Plunge into cold water and peel the skin away from the cross.
Note: Green olives are picked and processed when they are unripe.

Thinly slice the capsicum, onion and celery. Finely chop the garlic.

Leave to simmer for 20 minutes, then season to taste with salt and pepper.

Add the sugar, vinegar, olives and capers to the pan and mix well.

ASPARAGUS WITH PARMESAN

Preparation time: 15 minutes
Total cooking time: 10 minutes
Serves 4

60 g (2 oz) butter
2 tablespoons grated fresh Parmesan
½ cup (40 g/1⅓ oz) fresh
    breadcrumbs
2 tablespoons pine nuts, chopped

1 clove garlic, finely chopped
2 teaspoons chopped fresh oregano
2 teaspoons chopped fresh
    flat-leaf parsley
freshly ground black pepper
500 g (1 lb) fresh asparagus
60 g (2 oz) butter, melted, for serving

1 Heat the butter in a pan and, when foaming, add the Parmesan cheese, breadcrumbs and pine nuts. Stir over medium heat until lightly browned and crisp, then add the garlic, herbs and pepper and mix well.

2 Boil, steam or microwave the asparagus for 2–3 minutes, or until just tender, then rinse under cold water and pat dry with paper towels.
3 Serve the asparagus immediately, sprinkled with the crisp Parmesan topping and drizzled with extra melted butter.

COOK'S FILE
Note: Use slightly stale bread to make breadcrumbs in a processor.

Chop the pine nuts, garlic, fresh oregano and flat-leaf parsley.

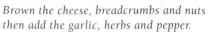

Brown the cheese, breadcrumbs and nuts then add the garlic, herbs and pepper.

It is easier to handle the asparagus if you keep them tied together during cooking.

Caponata (top) and Asparagus with Parmesan

MUSHROOMS IN TOMATO SAUCE

Preparation time: 15 minutes
Total cooking time: 20 minutes
Serves 4 as a side dish

2 tablespoons extra virgin
    olive oil
2 cloves garlic, sliced

600 g (1¼ lb) large button
    mushrooms, halved
2 tablespoons tomato paste
2 tablespoons chopped fresh marjoram
250 g (8 oz) cherry tomatoes, halved
freshly ground black pepper
1 tablespoon chopped fresh oregano
    leaves

1 Heat the oil in a pan, add the
garlic and stir over moderate heat for
1 minute; do not brown.

2 Add the mushrooms and cook,
stirring, for 5 minutes, until
combined and beginning to soften.
3 Stir through the tomato paste,
marjoram and cherry tomatoes and
cook over low heat until the
mushrooms are soft. Serve sprinkled
with pepper and oregano leaves.

COOK'S FILE
Note: Can be made up to 2 days ahead
and served hot or cold.

*Stir the garlic over medium heat until
fragrant but not browned.*

*Add the mushrooms to the pan and stir
until they begin to soften.*

*Cook over low heat until the mushrooms
are soft.*

FENNEL WITH PECORINO CHEESE

Preparation time: 15 minutes
Total cooking time: 25 minutes
Serves 4

4 fennel bulbs
1 clove garlic, crushed
½ lemon, sliced

2 tablespoons olive oil
1 teaspoon salt
3 tablespoons butter, melted
2 tablespoons grated pecorino cheese

1 Cut the top shoots and base off the fennel and remove the tough outer layers. Cut into segments and place in a pan with the garlic, lemon, oil and salt. Cover with water and bring to the boil. Reduce the heat and simmer for 20 minutes, or until just tender.

2 Drain well and place in a heatproof dish. Drizzle with the butter. Sprinkle with the cheese and season with salt and pepper to taste.
3 Place under a preheated grill until the cheese has browned. Best served immediately.

COOK'S FILE
Note: If pecorino (a hard sheeps milk cheese) is not available, then use Parmesan instead.

Trim the tops and bases from the fennel and remove the tough outer layers.

Place the fennel, garlic, lemon, oil and salt in a pan.

Sprinkle grated pecorino cheese over the fennel and brown under a grill.

STUFFED CAPSICUMS

Preparation time: 20 minutes
Total cooking time: 45 minutes
Serves 4–6

1 tablespoon olive oil
1 onion, finely chopped
1 clove garlic, crushed
3 rashers rindless bacon, finely
    chopped
150 g risoni, cooked
1 cup freshly grated mozzarella
    cheese
½ cup freshly grated Parmesan
    cheese
2 tablespoons chopped fresh parsley
4 large red capsicum, halved
    lengthwise, seeds removed
425 g can tomatoes
½ cup dry white wine
1 tablespoon tomato paste
½ teaspoon ground oregano
salt and freshly ground black pepper,
    to taste
2 tablespoons chopped fresh basil

1 Preheat oven to moderate 180°C.
Lightly oil a large shallow ovenproof
dish. Heat oil in a pan. Add onion and
garlic; stir over low heat until onion
is tender. Add bacon; stir until crisp.
2 Transfer bacon mixture to large
bowl and combine with risoni,
cheeses and parsley. Spoon mixture
into capsicum halves. Arrange in dish.
3 In bowl, combine undrained,
crushed tomatoes, wine, tomato
paste, oregano, salt and pepper.
Spoon over risoni mixture. Sprinkle
with basil. Bake for 35–40 minutes.

COOK'S FILE
Hint: Serve with baked chicken.

STUFFED MUSHROOM SALAD

Preparation time: 25 minutes
Total cooking time: Nil
Serves 4

20 button mushrooms
¼ cup (60 g/2 oz) pesto, chilled
100 g (3¼ oz) rocket leaves
1 green oakleaf lettuce
12 small black olives
⅓ cup (50 g/1¾ oz) sliced semi-dried
   or sun-dried tomatoes
1 tablespoon coarsely chopped basil
Parmesan shavings, to serve

DRESSING
⅓ cup (80 ml/2¾ fl oz) olive oil
1 tablespoon white wine vinegar
1 teaspoon Dijon mustard

1 Trim the mushroom stalks level with the caps and scoop out the remaining stalk using a melon baller. Spoon the pesto into the mushrooms.
2 To make the Dressing, place the ingredients in a small bowl and whisk to combine. Season with salt and pepper, to taste.
3 Arrange the rocket and lettuce leaves on a serving plate and top with the mushrooms, olives, tomato and basil. Drizzle the dressing over the salad and top with the Parmesan shavings. Serve immediately.

COOK'S FILE
Hint: Homemade pesto is preferable for this recipe. To make your own, process 1 cup (30 g/1 oz) loosely packed basil leaves, 2 tablespoons pine nuts and ¼ cup (25 g/¾ oz) grated Parmesan in a food processor to form a smooth paste. Gradually pour in ¼ cup (60 ml/2 fl oz) olive oil in a steady stream with the motor running. Process until combined. Note: Semi sun-dried tomatoes are brighter and more succulent than sun-dried tomatoes, giving your salad more colour.

Draw a vegetable peeler across a block of Parmesan to make the shavings.

Trim the mushroom stalks so they are level with the caps.

Spoon the chilled pesto into the mushroom caps.

ITALIAN PEAR SALAD

Preparation time: 20 minutes
Total cooking time: Nil
Serves 4

4 ripe green or red pears
250 g (8 oz) bocconcini, sliced
4 thin slices prosciutto, cut into bite-
    sized pieces
4 fresh figs, quartered
¼ cup (30 g/1 oz) walnut pieces

DRESSING
¼ cup (60 ml/2 fl oz) extra
    virgin olive oil
¼ teaspoon finely grated
    lemon rind
1 tablespoon lemon juice
1 tablespoon chopped chives

1 Cut the pears into quarters and use a melon baller or teaspoon to remove the cores. Arrange the pears in a serving dish and scatter with the sliced bocconcini, prosciutto, figs and walnut pieces.

2 To make the Dressing, put the oil, lemon rind and juice, and chives in a small bowl and whisk to combine. Season with salt and pepper, to taste. Drizzle the dressing over the salad and serve immediately.

COOK'S FILE
Note: If fresh figs are unavailable or out of season, use dried figs.

Using a large sharp knife, cut each bocconcini into about 4 slices.

Using a sharp knife, cut the fresh figs into quarters.

Cut the pears into quarters and use a melon baller to remove the cores.

ASPARAGUS AND MUSHROOM SALAD

Preparation time: 20 minutes
Total cooking time: 10 minutes
Serves 4

155 g asparagus spears
1 tablespoon wholegrain mustard
¼ cup (60 ml) orange juice
2 tablespoons lemon juice
1 tablespoon lime juice
1 tablespoon orange zest
2 teaspoons lemon zest

2 teaspoons lime zest
2 cloves garlic, crushed
1¼ cup (90 g) honey
400 g button mushrooms, halved
150 g rocket
1 red capsicum, cut into strips

1 Trim the woody ends from the asparagus spears and cut in half on the diagonal. Place in a saucepan of boiling water and cook for 1 minute, or until just tender. Drain, plunge into cold water and set aside.
2 Place the mustard, citrus juice and zest, garlic and honey in a large saucepan and season with pepper.

Bring to the boil, then reduce the heat and add the mushrooms, tossing for 2 minutes. Cool.
3 Remove the mushrooms from the sauce with a slotted spoon. Return the sauce to the heat, bring to the boil, then reduce the heat and simmer for 3–5 minutes, or until reduced and syrupy. Cool slightly.
4 Toss the mushrooms, rocket leaves, capsicum and asparagus. Place on a plate and drizzle with the sauce.

Use a zester to remove the zest of the orange, lemon and lime.

Toss the mushrooms in the mustard, juices, zest, garlic and honey.

Simmer the sauce until it is reduced and syrupy.

INSALATA CAPRESE
(Tomato and bocconcini salad)

Preparation time: 10 minutes
Total cooking time: Nil
Serves 4

3 large vine-ripened tomatoes
250 g bocconcini (see Note)
12 fresh basil leaves
¼ cup (60 ml) extra virgin olive oil
4 basil leaves, roughly torn, extra,
    optional

1 Slice the tomatoes into 1 cm slices,
making twelve slices altogether. Slice
the bocconcini into twenty-four
1 cm slices.
2 Arrange the tomato slices on a
serving plate, alternating them with
2 slices of bocconcini. Interleave the

basil leaves between the slices of
bocconcini.
3 Drizzle with the oil, sprinkle with
the basil, if desired, and season well
with salt and ground black pepper.

COOK'S FILE
Note: This popular summer salad is
most successful with very fresh buffalo
mozzarella if you can find it. We've used
bocconcini in this recipe as it can be
difficult to find very fresh mozzarella.

Slice the bocconcini into twenty-four
1 cm thick slices.

Arrange the tomato slices on a serving
plate, alternating with the bocconcini.

TUNA AND WHITE BEAN SALAD

Preparation time: 25 minutes
Total cooking time: 5 minutes
Serves 4–6

400 g tuna steaks
1 small red onion, thinly sliced
1 tomato, seeded and chopped
1 small red capsicum, thinly sliced
2 x 400 g cans cannellini beans
2 cloves garlic, crushed
1 teaspoon chopped fresh thyme
4 tablespoons finely chopped fresh
    flat-leaf parsley

1½ tablespoons lemon juice
⅓ cup (80 ml) extra virgin
    olive oil
1 teaspoon honey
olive oil, for brushing
100 g rocket leaves
1 teaspoon lemon zest

1 Place the tuna steaks on a plate, sprinkle with cracked black pepper on both sides, cover with plastic and refrigerate until needed.
2 Combine the onion, tomato and capsicum in a large bowl. Rinse the cannellini beans under cold running water for 30 seconds, drain and add to the bowl with the garlic, thyme and 3 tablespoons of the parsley.

3 Place the lemon juice, oil and honey in a small saucepan, bring to the boil, then simmer, stirring, for 1 minute, or until the honey dissolves. Remove from the heat.
4 Brush a barbecue or chargrill with olive oil, and heat until very hot. Cook the tuna for 1 minute on each side. The meat should still be pink in the middle. Slice into 3 cm cubes and combine with the salad. Pour on the warm dressing and toss well.
5 Place the rocket on a platter. Top with the salad, season and garnish with the zest and parsley. Serve.

Add the beans, garlic, thyme and parsley to the bowl and mix well.

Heat the lemon juice, honey and oil in a saucepan until the honey dissolves.

Cook the tuna until still pink in the middle, and cut into 3 cm cubes.

161

FARFALLE SALAD WITH SUN-DRIED TOMATOES AND SPINACH

Preparation time: 20 minutes
Total cooking time: 12 minutes
Serves 4–6

500 g farfalle (butterfly pasta) or spiral pasta
3 spring onions
50 g sun-dried tomatoes, cut in strips
1 bunch English spinach, stalks trimmed and leaves shredded
⅓ cup toasted pine nuts
1 tablespoon chopped fresh oregano

DRESSING
¼ cup olive oil
1 teaspoon fresh chopped chilli
1 clove garlic, crushed
salt and pepper, to taste

1 Add pasta to a large pan of rapidly boiling water and cook until just tender. Drain pasta and rinse well under cold water. Transfer to a large salad bowl. Trim spring onions and chop finely. Add to pasta with tomato, spinach, pine nuts and oregano.
2 To make Dressing: Combine oil, chilli, garlic, salt and pepper in a small screwtop jar and shake well.
3 Pour dressing over the top of salad; toss well and serve.

COOK'S FILE
Storage time: Serve immediately.

1

2

3

PROSCIUTTO, MIXED CRESS AND EGG SALAD

Preparation time: 20 minutes
Total cooking time: 10 minutes
Serves 4

3 eggs
250 g (8 oz) watercress
1 baby fennel bulb, thinly sliced
1 leek, thinly sliced
25 g (¾ oz) mustard cress
80 g (2¾ oz) thinly sliced prosciutto, trimmed and cut into wide strips

DRESSING
⅓ cup (80 ml/2¾ fl oz) extra virgin olive oil
½ teaspoon finely grated orange rind
2 tablespoons orange juice
3 teaspoons wholegrain mustard

1 Cook the eggs in a pan of simmering water for 8 minutes. Drain and cool briefly under cold running water and then leave in a bowl of cold water for 15 minutes. Shell and cut into quarters.
2 Trim the coarse stems from the watercress and combine with the fennel and leek slices on a serving plate or in a shallow bowl. Toss two-thirds of the mustard cress with the prosciutto and arrange over the greens. Top with the egg quarters, then sprinkle with the remaining mustard cress.
3 To make the Dressing: Mix all the ingredients together well, then season to taste with salt and freshly ground black pepper. Drizzle over the salad and serve.

Thinly slice the baby fennel bulb, discarding the green tops.

Trim and discard the coarse stems from the watercress.

Season the dressing with freshly ground black pepper.

DESSERTS

CHILLED ORANGE CREAMS

Preparation time: 30 minutes
+ chilling
Total cooking time: 5 minutes
Serves 6

½ cup (125 ml/4 fl oz) juice of blood oranges
3 teaspoons gelatine
4 egg yolks
½ cup (125 g/4 oz) caster sugar
1¼ cups (315 ml/10 fl oz) milk
1 teaspoon finely grated blood orange rind
1 cup (250 ml/8 fl oz) cream

1 Put a large bowl in the freezer and chill. Put a few drops of almond or light olive oil on your fingertips and lightly grease the insides of six ½-cup (125 ml/4 fl oz) moulds. Put the orange juice in a small bowl and sprinkle with gelatine; set aside.
2 Whisk the yolks and sugar in a small bowl until thick. Heat the milk and rind in a pan and gradually pour onto the egg mixture while whisking. Return to the pan and stir until the custard coats the back of the spoon —do not allow it to boil. Add the gelatine mixture and stir to dissolve.
3 Pour the mixture immediately through a strainer into the chilled bowl. Cool, stirring occasionally, until beginning to thicken. Whip the cream into soft peaks and fold into the custard. Spoon into the moulds and chill to set. Serve with cream, if liked.

COOK'S FILE
Storage time: Eat within 24 hours.

Put the blood orange juice in a small bowl and sprinkle with gelatine.

Stir the custard until it will coat the back of a spoon.

Pour the custard mixture through a strainer into the chilled bowl.

Whip the cream into soft peaks and then fold into the custard with a metal spoon.

Cut the slab sponge cake into 12 curved pieces with a sharp knife.

Put the thin ends of the cake slices in the centre so they fit together neatly.

Spoon the chocolate and hazelnut cream into the centre cavity and pack firmly.

Make a cardboard template and enlist help to give the Zuccotto a fancy finish.

COOK'S FILE
Best made a day in advance to give the flavours time to develop while chilling.

ZUCCOTTO

Preparation time: 1 hour + chilling
Total cooking time: Nil
Serves 6–8

1 slab sponge cake, about
    30 x 25 cm (12 x 10 inches)
⅓ cup (80 ml/2¾ fl oz) Kirsch
3 tablespoons Cointreau
⅓ cup (80 ml/2¾ fl oz) rum, Cognac,
    Grand Marnier or maraschino
2 cups (500 ml/16 fl oz) cream
90 g (3 oz) dark roasted almond
    chocolate, chopped
¾ cup (165 g/5½ oz) finely chopped
    mixed glacé fruit
100 g (3⅓ oz) dark chocolate, melted
70 g (2⅓ oz) roasted hazelnuts,
    chopped
cocoa powder and icing sugar, to
    decorate

1 Line a 6-cup (1.5 litre) pudding basin with damp muslin. Cut the cake into 12 curved pieces with a sharp knife. Work with one strip of cake at a time, lightly brushing it with the combined liqueurs and arranging the pieces closely in the basin. Put the thin ends in the centre so the slices cover the base and side. Brush with the remaining liqueur to soak the cake. Chill.
2 Beat the cream into stiff peaks, then divide in half. Fold the almond chocolate and glacé fruit into one half. Spread evenly over the cake in the basin, leaving a space in the centre.
3 Fold the cooled melted chocolate and hazelnuts into the remaining cream and spoon into the centre, packing firmly. Smooth the surface, cover and refrigerate overnight to allow the cream to firm slightly.
4 Turn out onto a serving plate and decorate by dusting generously with cocoa powder and icing sugar. You can make a cardboard template to help you dust separate wedges neatly, although you may need help holding it in place. Serve immediately, as the cream mixture will soften quickly.

FROZEN ZABAGLIONE WITH MARSALA SAUCE

Preparation time: 15 minutes
+ 6 hours freezing
Total cooking time: 10 minutes
Serves 4

⅔ cup (170 ml) cream
3 egg yolks
½ teaspoon vanilla essence
¾ cup (185 ml) Marsala
⅓ cup (90 g) caster sugar
⅓ cup (50 g) whole blanched
   almonds, toasted and chopped

1 Whip the cream to firm peaks, cover and refrigerate until needed.
2 Place the egg yolks, vanilla, ½ cup (125 ml) of the Marsala and half of the sugar in a non-metallic bowl and whisk well.
3 Fill one-third of a saucepan with water and bring to a simmer over medium heat. Sit the bowl on top of the saucepan, making sure the base of the bowl does not touch the water. Whisk continuously for 5 minutes, or until thick and foamy. The mixture should hold its form when you drizzle some from the whisk.
4 Remove from the heat and stand in a bowl of ice, whisking for 3 minutes, or until cool. Remove from the ice, then gently fold in the whipped cream and almonds. Carefully pour into four ½ cup (125 ml) dariole moulds or ramekins, cover with plastic wrap and freeze for 6 hours, or until firm.
5 Combine the remaining Marsala and sugar in a small saucepan and stir over low heat until the sugar dissolves. Bring just to the boil, then reduce the heat and simmer for 4–5 minutes, or until just syrupy— do not overcook or the syrup will harden when cool. Remove from the heat and set aside until needed
6 Briefly dip the moulds into warm water, then loosen with a knife. Turn out onto a plate and drizzle with sauce. Garnish with almonds, if desired.

Whisk the egg mixture continuously until thick and foamy.

Fold the whipped cream and chopped almonds into the egg mixture.

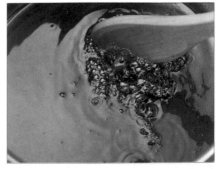

Simmer the Marsala sauce until just syrupy, then remove from the heat.

CASSATA

Preparation time: 50 minutes
+ overnight freezing
Total cooking time: Nil
Serves 20

FIRST LAYER
2 eggs, separated
⅓ cup icing sugar
¾ cup cream
50 g flaked almonds, toasted
almond essence

SECOND LAYER
130 g dark chocolate, chopped
1 tablespoon dark cocoa
2 eggs, separated
⅓ cup icing sugar
¾ cup thickened or pouring cream

THIRD LAYER
2 eggs, separated
¼ cup icing sugar
1 cup thickened or pouring cream
60 g glacé cherries, halved
2 tablespoons chopped preserved
    ginger
220 g glacé fruit (pineapple, apricot,
    fig and peach), finely chopped
1 teaspoon vanilla essence

1 Line base and sides of a deep 20 cm square tin with foil. To make first layer: Beat egg whites with electric beaters until soft peaks form. Add the icing sugar gradually, beating well after each addition. In a separate bowl, beat cream until firm peaks form. Using a metal spoon, fold yolks and beaten egg whites into cream. Add almonds and a few drops of essence. Stir until combined. Spoon into tin; smooth surface. Tap tin gently on bench to level surface of mixture. Freeze 30–60 minutes, or until firm.

2 To make second layer: Place chocolate in heatproof bowl over pan of simmering water; stir until melted. Add cocoa, stir until smooth. Remove from heat, cool slightly. Proceed as for step 1, beating egg whites, icing sugar and then cream. Using a metal spoon, fold chocolate into cream. Fold in yolks and beaten egg whites, stir until smooth. Spoon over frozen first layer. Tap tin on bench to level surface. Freeze 30–60 minutes, until firm.

3 To make third layer: Proceed as for step 1, beating egg whites, icing sugar and then cream. With metal spoon, fold yolks and egg white into cream; stir in fruit and essence. Spoon over chocolate layer in tin. Freeze overnight. Slice and serve. Wrap the remainder in foil and return to freezer.

COOK'S FILE
Storage time: Store for up to 1 week, tightly wrapped, in freezer.

1

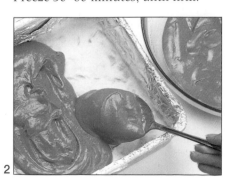

2

3

Press the pastry into the base with your fingertips.

Line with baking paper and then fill with dried beans or rice to bake blind.

Push the ricotta through a sieve and then beat together with the sugar.

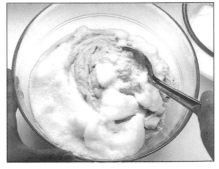

Fold the beaten egg white into the ricotta mixture with a metal spoon.

SICILIAN CHEESECAKE

Preparation time: 45 minutes
+ chilling
Total cooking time: 1 hour
25 minutes
Serves 8

2 cups (250 g/8 oz) plain flour
160 g (5¼ oz) butter, chopped
¼ cup (60 g/2 oz) caster sugar
1 teaspoon grated lemon rind
1 egg, lightly beaten

RICOTTA FILLING
½ cup (60 g/2 oz) raisins, chopped
⅓ cup (80 ml/2¾ fl oz) Marsala
500 g (1 lb) fresh ricotta
½ cup (125 g/4 oz) caster sugar
1 tablespoon plain flour
4 eggs, separated
½ cup (125 ml/4 fl oz) cream

1 Lightly grease a 26 cm (10½-inch) round springform tin. Sift the flour and a pinch of salt into a large bowl, rub in the butter. Add sugar, rind, egg and a little water if needed and, using a knife, cut through to form a rough dough. Press into a ball.
2 Roll out dough on a lightly floured surface to line the base and side of tin; chill for 30 minutes. Preheat oven to moderately hot 190°C (375°F/Gas 5). Prick the pastry base, line with baking paper and fill with dried beans or rice. Bake for 15 minutes, remove the beans and paper and bake for 8 minutes, or until pastry is dry. If the base puffs up, gently press down with the beans in the paper. Allow to cool. Reduce oven to warm 160°C (315°F/Gas 2–3).
3 To make Filling: Put raisins and Marsala in a bowl, cover and leave to soak. Push ricotta through a sieve. Beat ricotta and caster sugar with a wooden spoon to combine. Add flour and egg yolks, then the cream and undrained raisins and mix well. In a small bowl, beat the egg whites until soft peaks form and gently fold into the ricotta mixture in two batches.
4 Pour filling into pastry case and bake for 1 hour, or until just set. Check while cooking and cover with foil if the pastry is overbrowning. Cool a little in the oven with the door ajar to prevent sinking. Serve warm with whipped cream.

STUFFED FIGS

Preparation time: 20 minutes
Total cooking time: 5 minutes
Makes 15

50 g (1⅔ oz) blanched almonds
15 soft dried figs
⅓ cup (60 g/2 oz) mixed peel
100 g (3⅓ oz) marzipan, chopped

1 Preheat oven to moderate 180°C (350°F/Gas 4). Place the almonds on an oven tray and bake for 5 minutes, until lightly golden. Leave to cool.
2 Remove the hard stem ends from the figs. Cut a cross in the top of each fig halfway through to the base and open out like petals.
3 Place the mixed peel and almonds in a food processor and process until fine. Add the marzipan and process in short bursts until fine and crumbly.

4 With your hands, press 2 teaspoons of marzipan filling together to make a ball. Place a ball inside each fig and press into shape around it. Serve at room temperature with coffee.

COOK'S FILE
Variation: Dip the bases of the figs into melted chocolate.
Storage time: Store figs in a single layer in a covered container in the refrigerator for up to 2 days.

Cut away the hard stem end from the bottom of each fig.

Cut a cross in the top and open out each fig like the petals of a flower.

Place a ball of marzipan filling in each fig and then remould the fruit around it.

RICOTTA POTS WITH RASPBERRIES

Preparation time: 20 minutes
Total cooking time: 25 minutes
Serves 4

4 eggs, separated
½ cup (125 g/4 oz) caster sugar
350 g (11¼ oz) fresh ricotta
¼ cup (35 g/1¼ oz) finely chopped
   pistachio nuts
1 teaspoon grated lemon rind

2 tablespoons lemon juice
1 tablespoon vanilla sugar (see Note)
200 g (6½ oz) fresh raspberries

1 Preheat the oven to moderate 180°C (350°F/Gas 4). Beat egg yolks and sugar in a small bowl until pale and creamy. Transfer to a large bowl and add the ricotta, pistachio nuts, lemon rind and juice and mix well.
2 In a separate bowl, whisk the egg whites into stiff peaks. Beat in the vanilla sugar, then fold into the ricotta mixture, stirring until just combined.

3 Lightly grease 4 individual, 1-cup (250 ml/8 fl oz) ramekins. Divide the raspberries among the dishes and spoon the ricotta filling over the top. Place on an oven tray and bake for 20–25 minutes, or until puffed and lightly browned. Serve immediately, dusted with a little icing sugar.

COOK'S FILE
Note: You can buy ready-made vanilla sugar or make your own. Split a vanilla bean in half lengthways and place in a jar of caster sugar (about 1 kg/2 lb). Leave for at least 4 days before using.

Beat together the egg yolks and sugar until pale and creamy.

Fold in the egg whites with a metal spoon, trying to keep the volume.

Put the raspberries in the ramekins and spoon the ricotta filling over the top.

HAZELNUT PUDDINGS WITH CHOCOLATE CREAM SAUCE AND HONEY ZABAGLIONE

Preparation time: 40 minutes
Total cooking time: 40 minutes
Serves 8

30 g (1 oz) butter, melted
½ cup (55 g/1¾ oz) ground hazelnuts
125 g (4 oz) butter
½ cup (125 g/4 oz) caster sugar
3 eggs, lightly beaten
2 cups (250 g/8 oz) self-raising flour, sifted
½ cup (60 g/2 oz) sultanas
⅓ cup (80 ml/2¾ fl oz) brandy
⅓ cup (80 ml/2¾ fl oz) buttermilk
white chocolate shavings, to decorate

CHOCOLATE CREAM SAUCE
1 cup (250 ml/8 fl oz) cream
30 g (1 oz) butter
200 g (6½ oz) dark chocolate, chopped

HONEY ZABAGLIONE
3 large egg yolks
3 tablespoons honey
2 tablespoons brandy
½ cup (125 ml/4 fl oz) cream

1 Preheat the oven to moderate 180°C (350°F/Gas 4). Brush eight, ½-cup (125 ml/4 fl oz) ovenproof ramekins with melted butter and coat with the ground hazelnuts, shaking off the excess. Beat together the butter and sugar with electric beaters until light and creamy. Add the eggs gradually, beating well after each addition. Fold in the flour, sultanas, brandy and buttermilk.

Spoon into the ramekins, cover with greased foil and secure with string.
2 Place the puddings in a large baking dish and pour in enough water to come three-quarters of the way up the sides of the ramekins. Bake for 25 minutes, topping up with more water if necessary. Test with a skewer before removing the ramekins from the pan—the skewer should come out clean when inserted into the centre of the pudding.
3 To make Chocolate Cream Sauce: Put the cream, butter and chocolate in a small pan and stir over low heat until melted and smooth. Remove from the heat and set aside.
4 To make Honey Zabaglione: Beat the egg yolks until thick and pale. Place the bowl over a pan of barely simmering water and beat in the honey. Beat for about 5 minutes, until thickened. Remove from the heat, cool to room temperature and stir in the brandy. Beat the cream in a small bowl until firm peaks form, then fold into the egg mixture.
5 Spread Chocolate Cream Sauce over half of each serving plate. Pour Zabaglione onto the other half. Unmould the warm pudding onto the centre of the plate and decorate with curls of white chocolate.

COOK'S FILE
Hint: Make chocolate shavings by simply running over the top of the chocolate block with a vegetable peeler. Or make chocolate curls by melting the chocolate and spreading in a thin layer over a cool smooth surface (such as a marble board). When the chocolate has set, scrape off curls with the edge of a sharp knife.

Brush the ramekins with melted butter then coat with ground hazelnuts.

Beat together the sugar and butter until light and creamy.

Cover the ramekins with foil and secure with string.

Pour water into the baking tray to make a bain-marie.

Put the bowl over a pan of simmering water and beat until thickened.

Unmould the puddings by working around the edges with a sharp knife.

ESPRESSO GRANITA

Preparation time: 20 minutes
+ freezing
Total cooking time: 5 minutes
Serves 6

¾ cup (185 g/6 oz) caster sugar
1½ tablespoons cocoa powder
5 cups (1.25 litres) freshly made,
 strong espresso coffee

whipped cream, to serve

1 Put the sugar and cocoa powder
in a large pan, gradually add ½ cup
(125 ml/4 fl oz) water and mix until
smooth. Bring to the boil, stirring
until the sugar dissolves. Reduce
the heat and simmer for 3 minutes.
2 Remove from the heat and add
the fresh coffee. Pour into a shallow
container or tray and allow to cool
completely. Freeze until partially set
and then stir with a fork to distribute

the ice crystals evenly. Freeze again
until firm.
3 Using a fork, work the Granita
into fine crystals and return to the
freezer for 1 hour before serving.
Spoon into glasses and serve
immediately, with whipped cream.

COOK'S FILE
Hint: Granita tends to freeze rock-hard
and can be quite difficult to break up if
frozen in a deep container.

*Put the sugar and cocoa powder in a
large pan and gradually add the water.*

*Remove the pan from the heat and pour
in the fresh coffee.*

*Use a fork to work the Granita into fine
crystals, then re-freeze for 1 hour.*

TIRAMISU

Preparation time: 30 minutes
+ 2 hours refrigeration
Total cooking time: Nil
Serves 6

3 cups (750 ml/24 fl oz) strong black
    coffee, cooled
3 tablespoons Marsala or
    coffee-flavoured liqueur
2 eggs, separated
3 tablespoons caster sugar
250 g (8 oz) mascarpone
1 cup (250 ml/8 fl oz) cream, whipped

16 large sponge fingers
2 tablespoons dark cocoa powder

1 Mix together the coffee and
Marsala in a bowl and set aside.
Using electric beaters, beat the
egg yolks and sugar in a bowl for
3 minutes, or until thick and pale.
Add the mascarpone and mix until
just combined. Transfer to a large
bowl and fold in the cream.
2 Beat the egg whites until soft peaks
form. Fold quickly and lightly into
the cream mixture.
3 Dip half the biscuits into the coffee
mixture, then drain off any excess
coffee and arrange in the base of a

2.5 litre ceramic dish. Spread half the
cream mixture over the biscuits.
4 Dip the remaining biscuits into
the remaining coffee mixture and
repeat the layers. Smooth the surface
and dust liberally with the cocoa
powder. Refrigerate for at least
2 hours, or until firm.

COOK'S FILE
Storage time: Tiramisu is best made a
day ahead to let the flavours develop.
Refrigerate until ready to serve.
Serving suggestion: Tiramisu is
delicious served with fresh fruit.

*Add the mascarpone to the egg yolks
and sugar and mix well.*

*Fold the beaten egg whites gently
into the cream mixture.*

*Dip half the biscuits in the coffee mixture,
drain, and arrange in the serving dish.*

CHOCOLATE MINT ICE-CREAM

Preparation time: 25 minutes
+ freezing
Total cooking time: 10 minutes
Serves 4–6

1 cup cream
¼ cup chopped fresh mint
100 g dark chocolate, broken
60 g milk chocolate, broken
2 eggs, lightly beaten

1 tablespoon caster sugar

Place cream and mint in a small pan. Stir over low heat until cream is almost boiling. Remove from heat; cool.
1 Add chocolate to the cream. Stir over low heat until chocolate has melted and mixture is smooth.
2 Whisk eggs and sugar in a small mixing bowl until creamy. Gradually add warm chocolate mixture through a strainer; discard the mint. Whisk until well combined. Cool.

3 Freeze mixture in an ice-cream machine according to the manufacturer's instructions. Alternatively, freeze in a metal container until ice-cream is just firm around the edges. Remove from the freezer, transfer mixture to large mixing bowl. Using an electric mixer, beat for 1 minute. Return to container and freeze overnight. Serve with fresh berries, if desired.

COOK'S FILE
Storage time: Ice-cream can be stored in the freezer for up to 3 weeks.

BELLINI SORBET

Preparation time: 20 minutes
+ freezing
Total cooking time: 2 minutes
Serves 6

2 cups caster sugar
4 cups water
5 large peaches
¾ cup Champagne
2 egg whites

1 Combine sugar and water in large
pan. Stir over medium heat without
boiling until sugar has dissolved.
Bring to the boil, add peaches and
simmer for 20 minutes. Remove
peaches from pan with a slotted
spoon and cool completely. Remove
1 cup of the poaching liquid.
2 Peel skin from the peaches.
Remove stones and cut flesh into
chunks. Place in food processor and
process until smooth. Add reserved
liquid and Champagne and process
briefly until combined.
3 Pour mixture into a shallow metal
tray and freeze until just firm—about
6 hours. Transfer mixture to a large
mixing bowl. Using electric beaters,
beat until smooth.
4 Beat egg whites until soft peaks
form. Using a metal spoon, gently
fold beaten egg white into sorbet
mixture. Return to metal tray and
freeze until firm. Serve sorbet in
scoops, with sliced fresh peaches and
dessert wafers, if desired.

COOK'S FILE
Storage time: Sorbet may be made up
to 2 days in advance; cover tightly.
Hint: To make sorbet in an ice-cream
churn, pour mixture into machine after
adding Champagne and churn until
beginning to freeze. Add beaten egg
white, continue churning until ready. It
will be slow to freeze due to the amount
of alcohol and sugar.
Note: Don't be tempted to use cheap
Champagne or "sparkling wine" for this
recipe—the difference will be noticeable.
Use a wine of the same quality you
would choose to drink.
Variation: Soft stone fruits, like plums or
nectarines, can also be used for sorbet.

PANNA COTTA WITH RUBY SAUCE

Preparation time: 20 minutes
+ chilling
Total cooking time: 20 minutes
Serves 6

1½ cups (375 ml/12 fl oz) milk
3 teaspoons gelatine
1½ cups (375 ml/12 fl oz) cream
⅓ cup (90 g/3 oz) caster sugar
2 tablespoons Amaretto liqueur

RUBY SAUCE
1 cup (250 g/8 oz) caster sugar
1 cinnamon stick
1 cup fresh or frozen raspberries
½ cup (125 ml/4 fl oz) good-quality
   red wine

1 Use your fingertips to lightly smear the inside of 6 individual 150 ml (5 fl oz) moulds with almond or light olive oil. Place 3 tablespoons of the milk in a small bowl and sprinkle with gelatine; leave to dissolve for a few minutes.
2 Put the remaining milk in a pan with the cream and sugar and heat gently while stirring, until almost boiling. Remove the pan from the heat; whisk the gelatine into the cream mixture and whisk until dissolved. Leave to cool for 5 minutes and then stir in the Amaretto.
3 Pour the mixture into the moulds and chill until set (about 4 hours). Unmould and serve with Ruby Sauce.
4 To make Ruby Sauce: Place the sugar and 1 cup (250 ml/8 fl oz) water in a pan and stir over medium heat until the sugar has completely dissolved (do not allow to boil). Add the cinnamon stick and simmer for 5 minutes. Add the raspberries and wine and boil rapidly for 5 minutes. Remove the cinnamon stick and push the sauce through a sieve; discard the seeds. Cool and then chill the sauce in the refrigerator before serving.

COOK'S FILE
Note: If you prefer, replace the Amaretto with ½ teaspoon of almond extract. The Panna Cotta will be a little firmer. This is delicious, and traditionally Italian, with fresh figs.

Put some of the milk into a small bowl and sprinkle with gelatine.

Whisk the dissolved gelatine into the cream mixture until dissolved.

Pour the mixture into the moulds and then refrigerate until set.

Remove the cinnamon stick and strain the sauce through a sieve.

MACERATED FRUITS WITH MASCARPONE

Preparation time: 20 minutes
Total cooking time: 10 minutes
Serves 4–6

2 oranges
1 cup raspberries
1 cup blueberries
2 tablespoons caster sugar
⅓ cup water
2 tablespoons sugar

1 Place each orange on a board and cut a 2 cm-wide slice from each end—cut down to where pulp starts. Remove the rind in wide strips, including all the pith and white membrane. Using a small, sharp knife, cut pith from rind and discard; cut the rind into thin strips.
2 Separate orange segments by carefully cutting between membrane and flesh. Combine orange segments and berries in a medium bowl, sprinkle with caster sugar and toss lightly. Cover and refrigerate.

3 Combine water and sugar in a small pan and stir over low heat without boiling until sugar has dissolved. Bring to the boil, reduce heat and add the orange rind. Simmer for 2 minutes until rind is tender; cool. Reserve 1 tablespoon of rind, combine syrup and rest of rind with berry mix. Spoon into goblets and garnish with reserved rind; serve with dollops of mascarpone.

COOK'S FILE
Fruit may be combined with syrup and refrigerated for up to 4 hours.

LEMON AND ALMOND TART

Preparation time: 40 minutes
+ chilling
Total cooking time: 1 hour
Serves 6–8

2 cups (250 g/8 oz) plain flour, sifted
¼ cup (60 g/2 oz) caster sugar
125 g (4 oz) butter, softened
1 teaspoon finely grated lemon rind
2 egg yolks

FILLING
350 g (11¼oz) fresh ricotta, sieved
⅓ cup (90 g/3 oz) caster sugar
3 eggs, well beaten
1 tablespoon grated lemon rind
½ cup (80 g/2⅔ oz) blanched
    almonds, finely chopped
3 tablespoons flaked almonds
icing sugar, to dust

1 Combine the flour, sugar and a pinch of salt in a large bowl. Make a well in the centre and add the butter, rind and yolks. Work the flour into the centre with the fingertips of one hand until a smooth dough forms (add a little more flour if necessary). Wrap in plastic wrap and chill for 1 hour.
2 To make Filling: Using electric beaters, beat the ricotta and sugar together. Add eggs gradually, beating well after each addition. Add the rind, beating briefly to combine, and then stir in the chopped almonds.
3 Preheat the oven to moderate 180°C (350°F/ Gas 4). Brush a 20 cm (8 inch) deep fluted flan tin with melted butter. Roll out the pastry on a lightly floured surface and line the prepared tin, removing the excess pastry. Pour in the filling and smooth the top. Sprinkle with the flaked almonds and bake for 55 minutes to 1 hour, or until lightly golden and set.

4 Cool to room temperature and carefully remove the sides from the tin. Dust with icing sugar to serve at room temperature or chilled.

For perfect pastry, use just your fingertips to bring the dough together.

Add the grated lemon rind and beat briefly to combine.

Roll a rolling pin over the lined tin to remove any excess pastry.

HONEY NUT ROLLS

Preparation time: 25 minutes
Total cooking time: 35 minutes
Serves 8

2 cups (250 g/8 oz) plain flour
¼ cup (60 g/2 oz) caster sugar
100 g (3⅓ oz) cold butter, chopped
4 tablespoons honey, warmed
3 tablespoons chopped almonds
3 tablespoons chopped pecans

1 teaspoon ground cinnamon
⅓ cup (60 g/2 oz) mixed peel, chopped
3 tablespoons chopped mixed almonds and pecans, extra

1 Preheat the oven to moderate 180°C (350°F/Gas 4). Put the flour, sugar, butter and a pinch of salt in a bowl. Rub in the butter until crumbly. Add 2–3 tablespoons cold water and cut through, until the mixture forms a dough. Gather together into a ball.

2 Cut dough in half and roll each piece into a strip 40 cm x 10 cm (16 x 4 inches). Trim the edges with a knife. Spread 3 tablespoons honey over the dough and sprinkle with nuts, cinnamon and mixed peel. Roll up lengthways into two long sausage shapes and cut these in four. Place on a greased or paper-lined baking tray.
3 Glaze with the remaining honey, sprinkle with mixed nuts and make diagonal slashes in the top. Bake for 35 minutes, or until golden brown. Serve warm with whipped cream.

Roll out each piece of dough into a long narrow strip.

Spread with honey, sprinkle with nuts, cinnamon and peel and then roll up.

Sprinkle with mixed nuts and then make a few diagonal slashes in the top.

LEMON SYRUP CAKE

Preparation time: 20 minutes
Total cooking time: 45 minutes
Serves 8

1 cup (125 g/4 oz) plain flour
¾ teaspoon baking powder
¼ teaspoon bicarbonate of soda
50 g (1⅔ oz) unsalted butter
½ cup (125 g/4 oz) caster sugar
2 eggs

⅓ cup (80 ml/2¾ fl oz) milk
3 tablespoons ground almonds
2 tablespoons grated lemon rind

SYRUP
100 g (3⅓ oz) caster sugar
⅓ cup (80 ml/2¾ fl oz) lemon juice

1 Preheat the oven to moderate 180°C (350°F/Gas 4). Grease and line a 20 cm (8 inch) springform tin. Sift the flour, baking powder, bicarbonate of soda and a pinch of salt into a bowl.

2 In a separate bowl, beat the butter, sugar and eggs until light and creamy (the mixture may appear curdled). Fold in the flour mixture, then gently stir in the milk, almonds and lemon rind. Spoon into the tin and bake for 30–35 minutes, or until a skewer comes out clean. Make holes in the top of the cake with the skewer.
3 To make Syrup: Put the sugar and lemon juice in a pan and stir over a low heat until syrupy; keep warm. Pour syrup over hot cake. Cool on a wire rack; turn out of tin to serve.

Fold in the flour mixture, then gently stir in the milk, almonds and lemon rind.

Use a skewer to make holes in the top of the cake so it absorbs the syrup.

Pour the syrup over the hot cake, so that it is absorbed. Cool before turning out.

GRILLED FIGS WITH AMARETTO MASCARPONE

Preparation time: 10 minutes
Total cooking time: 15 minutes
Serves 4

¼ cup (60 g) caster sugar
¼ cup (60 ml) cream
½ teaspoon vanilla essence
½ cup (110 g) mascarpone
50 ml Amaretto
1½ tablespoons caster sugar, extra
¼ cup (35 g) blanched almonds, finely chopped

½ teaspoon ground cinnamon
6 fresh figs, halved

1 Line a baking tray with foil. Place caster sugar and ¼ cup (60 ml) water in a small saucepan and stir over low heat until sugar has dissolved; brush down the side of the pan with a clean brush dipped in water if any crystals appear. Bring to the boil and cook, without stirring, for about 8 minutes, swirling occasionally until the mixture is golden. Quickly remove the pan from the heat and carefully pour in the cream, stirring constantly until smooth, then stir in the vanilla.
2 To make Amaretto Mascarpone: Place the mascarpone, Amaretto and

2 teaspoons of the extra caster sugar in a bowl and mix together well.
3 Combine the chopped almonds, cinnamon and remaining caster sugar on a plate.
4 Press the cut side of each fig half into the almond mixture, then place, cut-side-up, onto the baking tray. Cook under a hot grill for 4–5 minutes, or until the sugar has caramelised and the almonds are nicely toasted—watch carefully to prevent burning.
5 Arrange three fig halves on each plate, place a dollop of the Amaretto Mascarpone to the side and drizzle with the sauce.

Swirl occasionally until the mixture is evenly golden.

Press the cut side of the figs into the almond mixture.

Cook the figs until the almonds are toasted but not burnt.

POACHED PEARS IN SAFFRON CITRUS SYRUP

Preparation time: 10 minutes
Total cooking time: 30 minutes
Serves 4

1 vanilla bean, split
   lengthways
½ teaspoon firmly packed
   saffron threads
¾ cup (185 g) caster sugar
2 teaspoons grated lemon rind
4 pears, peeled

whipped cream, to serve
   (optional)
biscotti, to serve (optional)

1 Place the vanilla bean, saffron threads, sugar, lemon rind and 2 cups (500 ml) water in a large saucepan and mix together well. Heat, stirring, over low heat until the sugar has dissolved. Bring to the boil, then reduce to a gentle simmer.
2 Add the pears and cook, covered, for 12–15 minutes, or until tender when tested with a metal skewer. Turn the pears over with a slotted spoon halfway through cooking.

Once cooked, remove from the syrup with a slotted spoon.
3 Remove the lid and allow the Saffron Citrus Syrup to come to the boil. Cook for 8–10 minutes, or until the syrup has reduced by half and thickened slightly. Remove the vanilla bean and drizzle the syrup over the pears. Serve with whipped cream and a couple of pieces of biscotti.

COOK'S FILE
note: Biscotti are available in a wide variety of flavours. You can buy biscotti at gourmet food stores, delicatessens and good supermarkets.

Stir the Saffron Citrus Syrup until the sugar has dissolved.

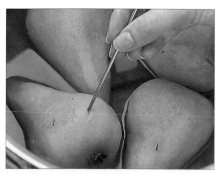

Cook the pears until tender when tested with a metal skewer.

Bring the Syrup to the boil and cook until slightly thickened.

HONEY AND PINE NUT TART

Preparation time: 25 minutes
+ 15 minutes refrigeration
Total cooking time: 1 hour
Serves 6

PASTRY
2 cups (250 g) plain flour
1½ tablespoons icing sugar
115 g chilled unsalted butter, chopped
1 egg, lightly beaten

FILLING
1½ cups (235 g) pine nuts
½ cup (175 g) honey
115 g unsalted butter, softened
½ cup (125 g) caster sugar
3 eggs, lightly beaten
¼ teaspoon vanilla essence
1 tablespoon almond liqueur
1 teaspoon finely grated lemon rind
1 tablespoon lemon juice
icing sugar, for dusting
crème fraîche or marscarpone, to serve

1 Preheat the oven to moderately hot 190°C (375°F/Gas 5) and place a baking tray on the middle shelf. Lightly grease a 23 cm x 3.5 cm deep loose-bottomed tart tin. To make the pastry, sift the flour and icing sugar into a large bowl and add the butter. Rub the butter into the flour with your fingertips until it resembles fine breadcrumbs. Make a well in the centre and add the egg and 2 tablespoons cold water. Mix with a flat-bladed knife, using a cutting action, until the mixture comes together in beads.
2 Gather the dough together and lift out onto a lightly floured work surface. Press the dough together into a ball, roll out to a circle 3 mm thick and invert into the tin. Use a small ball of pastry to press the pastry into the tin, allowing any excess to hang over the sides. Roll a rolling pin over the tin, cutting off any excess pastry. Prick the base all over with a fork and then chill for 15 minutes. Cut out 3 leaves about 4 cm long from the scraps for decoration. Cover and chill.

3 Line the pastry with baking paper and fill with pie weights or dried beans. Bake on the heated tray for 10 minutes, then remove.
4 Reduce the oven to moderate 180°C (350°F/Gas 4). To make the filling, spread the pine nuts on a baking tray and roast in the oven for 3 minutes, or until golden. Heat the honey in a small saucepan until runny. Beat the butter and sugar in a bowl until smooth and pale. Gradually add the eggs, beating well after each addition. Mix in the honey, vanilla, liqueur, lemon rind and juice and a pinch of salt. Stir in the pine nuts, spoon into the pastry case and smooth the surface. Arrange the reserved pastry leaves in the centre.
5 Place on the hot tray and bake for 40 minutes, or until golden and set. Cover the top with foil after 25 minutes. Serve warm or at room temperature, dusted with icing sugar. Serve with crème fraîche or mascarpone.

COOK'S FILE
Note: The filling rises and cracks during baking but settles down as the tart cools.

Use a small ball of pastry to press the pastry into the tin.

Arrange the reserved pastry leaves over the smoothed pine nut filling.

STRAWBERRY AND MASCARPONE TART

Preparation time: 45 minutes
+ 45 minutes refrigeration
Total cooking time: 30 minutes
Serves 6

PASTRY
1½ cups (185 g) plain flour
125 g unsalted butter, chilled and
    cut into cubes
⅓ cup (80 ml) iced water

FILLING
500 g strawberries, hulled and
    halved
2 teaspoons vanilla essence
50 ml Drambuie
⅓ cup (60 g) soft brown sugar
250 g mascarpone
300 ml thick cream
2 teaspoons orange zest

1 Sift the flour into a large bowl and add the butter. Rub the butter into the flour with your fingertips until it resembles fine breadcrumbs. Make a well in the centre and add almost all the water and mix with a flat-bladed knife, using a cutting action, until the mixture comes together in beads, adding the remaining water if needed. Gently gather the dough together and lift out onto a lightly floured surface.

2 Roll the dough out between two sheets of baking paper until it is large enough to line the base and side of a lightly greased 22 cm (3.5 cm deep) loose-bottomed flan tin. Ease the pastry into the tin and trim the edge, then chill for 15 minutes. Preheat the oven to moderately hot 200°C (400°F/ Gas 6) and heat a baking tray.

3 Line the pastry with a sheet of baking paper and pour in some baking beads or rice, then bake on the heated baking tray for 15 minutes.

Remove the paper and beads and bake for 10–15 minutes, or until dry and golden. Cool completely.

4 Meanwhile, place the strawberries, vanilla, Drambuie and 1 tablespoon of the brown sugar in a bowl and mix well. Place the mascarpone, cream, zest and remaining brown sugar in another bowl and mix. Cover both bowls and refrigerate for 30 minutes, tossing the strawberries once or twice.

5 Whip half the mascarpone cream until firm, then evenly spoon it into the tart shell. Drain the strawberries, reserving the liquid. Pile the strawberries onto the tart. Serve wedges of the tart with a drizzling of the reserved liquid and a dollop of the remaining mascarpone cream.

Mix with a flat-bladed knife until the mixture comes together in beads.

Remove the paper and baking beads from the pastry shell.

CHOCOLATE RICOTTA TART

Preparation time: 20 minutes
+ chilling
Total cooking time: 1 hour
Serves 8–10

1½ cups (185 g/6 oz) plain flour
100 g (3⅓ oz) cold butter, chopped
2 tablespoons caster sugar
1 tablespoon butter, melted

FILLING
1.25 kg (2½ lb) ricotta cheese
½ cup (125 g/4 oz) caster sugar
2 tablespoons plain flour
125 g (4 oz) chocolate, finely chopped

2 teaspoons coffee essence
4 egg yolks
40 g (1⅓ oz) chocolate, extra
½ teaspoon vegetable oil

1 Make sweet shortcrust pastry by sifting flour into a large bowl and adding the butter. Rub butter into the flour with your fingertips, until fine and crumbly. Stir in sugar. Add 3 tablespoons cold water and cut with a knife to form a dough, adding a little more water if necessary. Turn out onto a lightly floured surface and gather together into a ball. Brush a 25 cm (10 inch) springform tin with melted butter. Roll out the dough to line the tin, coming about two-thirds of the way up the side. Cover and refrigerate while making the filling.

2 To make Filling: Mix together the ricotta, sugar, flour and a pinch of salt until smooth. Stir in chocolate, coffee essence and yolks. Spoon into the chilled pastry shell and smooth. Chill for 30 minutes, or until firm. Preheat the oven to moderate 180°C (350°F/Gas 4).
3 Put the tin on a baking tray. Bake for 1 hour, or until firm. Leave to cool before removing the sides from the tin. Melt the extra chocolate and stir in the oil. With a fork, flick thin drizzles of melted chocolate over the tart. Cool completely before cutting.

COOK'S FILE
Note: The tart may crack during baking but this will not be noticeable when it cools and is decorated.

Have cool hands and use just your fingertips when rubbing butter into flour.

Do not knead the dough (it will become tough), just gather it into a ball.

Mix together the melted chocolate and oil and flick over the tart.

BAKING

ROSEMARY BREAD TRIOS

Preparation time: 40 minutes
+ 1 hour 40 minutes rising
Total cooking time: 15 minutes
Makes 10 trios

7 g (¼ oz) sachet dried yeast
1 teaspoon caster sugar
4 cups (500 g/1 lb) plain flour
1 tablespoon caster sugar, extra
1 teaspoon salt
1 cup (250 ml/8 fl oz) warm milk
¼ cup (60 ml/2 fl oz) vegetable oil
10 small sprigs of rosemary
1 egg yolk
sea salt flakes, to sprinkle

1 Combine the yeast, caster sugar and ½ cup (125 ml/4 fl oz) of warm water in a small bowl. Cover and set aside in a warm place for 10 minutes, or until frothy.
2 Sift the flour into a large bowl and stir in the extra caster sugar and salt. Make a well in the centre and pour in the warm milk, oil and frothy yeast. Mix to a soft dough, gather into a ball then turn out onto a lightly floured surface and knead for 10 minutes, or until smooth and elastic. Add a little extra flour if the dough becomes too sticky. Place in a large,

oiled bowl, cover loosely with greased plastic wrap and leave in a warm place for 1 hour, or until doubled in size.
3 Punch down the dough, then turn out onto a lightly floured surface and knead for 1 minute. Lightly grease 2 large baking trays. Divide the dough into 10 pieces. Form each piece into three balls—keeping the remaining pieces covered—and place close together on the prepared baking tray; add a sprig of rosemary onto the centre of each trio. Repeat with the remaining pieces of dough, and lay each set separately on the baking tray.
4 Cover the trios with a damp tea towel and set aside for 20 minutes, or until well risen. Preheat the oven to moderate 180°C (350°F/Gas 4). Brush the trios lightly with the combined egg yolk and 1 teaspoon of water and sprinkle with the sea salt flakes. Bake for 15 minutes, or until golden brown. Allow to cool on a wire rack and replace the rosemary sprigs with fresh ones, if you want.

COOK'S FILE
Note: 'Punching down' is when you knock the dough with your fist to expel the air.

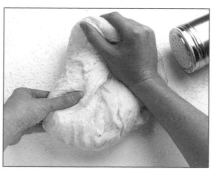

Knead the dough on a lightly floured surface until smooth and elastic.

Arrange the 3 balls together on a lightly greased baking tray.

FOCACCIA
(Italian flatbread)

Preparation time: 30 minutes
+ 3 hours 40 minutes rising
Total cooking time: 20 minutes
Makes two loaves

½ teaspoon caster sugar
7 g sachet dry yeast
1 kg bread flour (see Note)
¼ cup (60 ml) olive oil

1 Mix the sugar, dry yeast and
2 tablespoons warm water in a small
bowl. Leave in a warm place for
10 minutes, or until foamy. If it
doesn't foam the yeast is dead and
you will have to start again.
2 Place the flour in a large bowl with
2 teaspoons salt, and mix well. Add
2 tablespoons of the oil, the yeast
mixture and 3 cups (750 ml) warm
water. Mix with a wooden spoon
until the mixture comes together in
a loose dough, then turn out onto a
lightly floured surface. Start kneading
to form a soft, moist, non-sticky
dough, adding a little extra flour or
warm water as needed. Knead for
8 minutes, or until smooth.
3 Lightly oil a large bowl. Place the
dough in the bowl and roll it around.
Cut a cross on top with a sharp knife.
Cover the bowl with a tea towel and
leave in a dry, warm place for 1 hour
30 minutes, or until doubled in size.
4 Punch down the dough on a
lightly floured surface. Divide in half.
Roll one portion out to a 28 x 20 cm
rectangle. Use the heels of your
hands to work from the middle of
the dough outwards and shape into
a 38 x 28 cm rectangle.

5 Lightly oil a baking tray and dust
with flour. Place the dough in the
centre and slide the tray inside a
plastic bag. Leave in a dry, warm place
for 2 hours, or until doubled in size.
6 Preheat the oven to 220°C (425°F/
Gas 7). Brush the dough with some
olive oil and bake for 20 minutes, or
until golden. Transfer to a wire rack
to cool. Allow air to circulate under
the loaf to keep the crust crisp.
Repeat with remaining dough. Best
eaten within 6 hours of baking.

COOK'S FILE
Note: If bread flour is unavailable,
you can use plain flour. It requires
less water, so start by adding 1 cup
(250 ml) of the water in step 2, then
gradually add more to give a soft but
non-sticky dough. The bread will be
a denser texture.

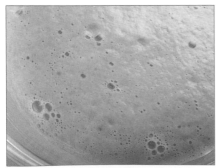

*Leave the yeast mixture in a warm place
until foamy.*

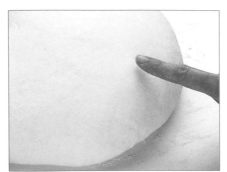

*Knead the dough until the impression
made by a finger springs out.*

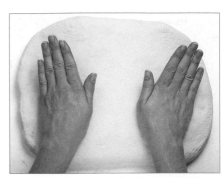

*Use the heels of your hands to work from
the middle outwards.*

SUN-DRIED TOMATO ROLLS

Preparation time: 20 minutes
+ resting
Total cooking time: 40 minutes
Makes 16 rolls

3 tablespoons olive oil
2 red onions, sliced
1 tablespoon tomato paste
⅔ cup (110 g/3⅔ oz) sun-dried
   tomatoes, chopped
1 tablespoon chopped fresh oregano
2 teaspoons chopped fresh rosemary
¼ teaspoon dried chilli flakes
14 g (½ oz) packet dried yeast
6 cups (750 g/1½ lb) plain flour
3 teaspoons salt
2 tablespoons polenta
1 egg white, lightly beaten

1 Heat the oil in a pan and cook the onions until very soft. Stir in the tomato paste, tomatoes, herbs and chilli. Cool to room temperature.
2 Put yeast, 1 cup (250 ml/8 fl oz) warm water and 1 cup (125 g/4 oz) of the flour in a bowl, then whisk until smooth and leave in a warm place for 20 minutes, or until frothy.
3 Sift remaining flour and salt into a bowl. Make a well in the centre and pour in yeast mix, 1 cup (250 ml/8 fl oz) warm water and the tomato mix. Mix to a soft sticky dough. Turn out onto a floured surface and knead for 5 minutes. Place in a greased bowl, cover loosely with greased plastic wrap and leave in a warm place for 1 hour, or until doubled. Grease two 20 cm (8 inch) round shallow cake tins and sprinkle with a little polenta.
4 Punch down dough, then knead on a floured surface for 3 minutes. Divide into 16 portions. Roll into balls and arrange in the cake tins. Make 2–3 cuts on top of each roll. Leave in a warm place for 20 minutes or until risen; brush with egg white and sprinkle with polenta. Preheat the oven to 200°C (400°F/Gas 6).
5 Bake for 30 minutes (cover with foil if overbrowning). For crusty rolls, spray with a little water about 3 times during baking. Turn out onto a wire rack and serve

Whisk the yeast, water and flour together and leave in a warm place until frothy.

Add the yeast mixture, warm water and tomato mixture to the flour.

Leave the dough in a warm place for 1 hour, or until doubled in size.

Divide the dough into 16 portions, then roll into balls and put in the tins.

Use the back of a large metal spoon to lightly crush the peppercorns.

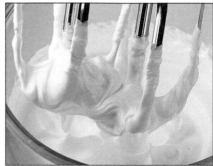

Beat the egg whites and caster sugar until the mixture turns white and thickens.

Fold the flour, spices, almonds and peppercorns into the egg white mixture.

Cut the bread into thin slices and arrange them in a single layer on baking trays.

PEPPER AND ALMOND BREAD

Preparation time: 10 minutes
+ 3 hours standing
Total cooking time: 1 hour
10 minutes
Makes about 70 pieces

2 teaspoons black peppercorns
2 egg whites
⅓ cup (90 g/3 oz) caster sugar
¾ cup (90 g/3 oz) plain flour
¼ teaspoon ground ginger
¼ teaspoon ground cinnamon
1 cup (155 g/5 oz) almonds

1 Preheat the oven to moderate 180°C (350°F/Gas 4). Grease an 8 x 26 cm (3 x 10½ inch) bar tin. Line the base and sides with baking paper. Lightly crush the peppercorns with the back of a metal spoon or in a mortar and pestle.

2 Beat the egg whites and sugar with electric beaters for 4 minutes, or until the mixture turns white and thickens. Sift the flour, ginger and cinnamon and fold in with the almonds and crushed peppercorns.

3 Spread the mixture into the tin. Bake for 35 minutes, or until lightly browned. Cool in the tin for at least 3 hours, before turning out onto a board. (You can wrap the bread in foil and slice the next day at this stage.) Using a serrated knife, cut the bread into 3 mm (⅛ inch) slices. Place the slices in a single layer on baking trays. Bake in a slow 150°C (300°F/Gas 2) oven for about 25–35 minutes, or until the slices are dry and crisp. Allow to cool completely before serving.

COOK'S FILE
Note: To make traditional almond bread, simply remove the peppercorns.

Stir the frothy yeast and oil into the flour and salt until well combined.

Flatten one portion of dough into a rectangle and put the basil and garlic on top.

Punch down the dough with your fist to expel the air.

Divide the dough into 12 portions and roll into sticks.

GRISSINI

Preparation time: 30 minutes
+ 1 hour 10 minutes standing
Total cooking time: 20 minutes
Makes 24

7 g (¼ oz) sachet dried yeast
1 teaspoon sugar
4 cups (500 g/1 lb) plain flour
¼ cup (60 ml/2 fl oz) olive oil
¼ cup (15 g/½ oz) chopped fresh basil
4 cloves garlic, crushed
½ cup (50 g/1¾ oz) finely grated
    Parmesan
2 teaspoons sea salt flakes
2 tablespoons finely grated
    Parmesan, extra

1 Combine the yeast, sugar and 1¼ cups (315 ml/10 fl oz) warm water in a small bowl and leave in a warm place for about 5–10 minutes, or until frothy. Sift the flour and 1 teaspoon salt into a bowl and stir in the frothy yeast and oil until the mixture is combined. Add more water if the dough is dry.
2 Gather the dough into a ball and turn out onto a lightly floured

surface. Knead for 10 minutes, or until soft and elastic. Divide the dough into two portions, add the basil and garlic to one portion, and the Parmesan to the other. The best way to do this is to flatten the dough into a rectangle and place the filling on top. Fold the dough to enclose the filling, then knead for a few minutes to incorporate evenly.
3 Place the doughs into two lightly oiled bowls and cover with plastic wrap. Leave in a warm place for about 1 hour, or until doubled in volume. Preheat the oven to very hot 230°C (450°F/Gas 8) and lightly grease two large baking trays.
4 Punch down the doughs and knead each again for 1 minute. Divide the two pieces of dough into 12 portions each, and roll each portion into a stick about 30 cm (12 inches) long and 5 mm (¼ inch) across. Place on the baking trays and brush with some water. Sprinkle the basil and garlic dough with the sea salt flakes, and the cheese dough with the extra Parmesan. Bake for 15 minutes, or until crisp and golden brown.

COOK'S FILE
Storage time: Grissini will keep stored in an airtight container for up to 1 week.

PARMESAN AND PROSCIUTTO LOAF

Preparation time: 30 minutes
+ 2 hours rising
Total cooking time: 25 minutes
Serves 6

7 g (¼ oz) dried yeast
1 teaspoon caster sugar
½ cup (125 ml/4 fl oz) warm milk
2 cups (250 g/8 oz) plain flour
1 teaspoon salt
1 egg, lightly beaten
30 g (1 oz) butter, melted and cooled
  slightly
1 tablespoon milk, extra

60 g (2 oz) sliced prosciutto, finely
  chopped
½ cup (35 g/1¼ oz) grated Parmesan

1 Grease a baking tray. Mix the yeast, sugar and milk in a bowl. Cover and set aside in a warm place for 10 minutes, or until frothy.
2 Mix the flour and salt in a bowl. Make a well in the centre and add the egg, butter and frothy yeast. Mix to a soft dough and gather into a ball; turn the dough out onto a floured surface and knead for 8 minutes, or until elastic.
3 Put in an oiled bowl, cover loosely with greased plastic wrap and leave in a warm place for 1¼ hours, or until doubled in size.

4 Punch down the dough, turn out onto a floured surface and knead for 30 seconds, or until smooth. Roll out to a rectangle, 30 x 20 cm (12 x 8 inches), and brush with some extra milk. Sprinkle with the prosciutto and Parmesan, leaving a border. Roll lengthways into a log shape.
5 Lay on the baking tray and brush with the remaining milk. Using a sharp knife, slash the loaf diagonally at intervals. Leave to rise in a warm place for 30 minutes. Preheat the oven to hot 220°C (425°F/Gas 7). Bake the loaf for 25 minutes, or until golden.

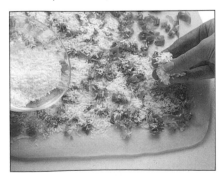

Sprinkle the prosciutto and Parmesan on the dough, leaving a clear border.

Roll up the dough tightly lengthways into a log shape.

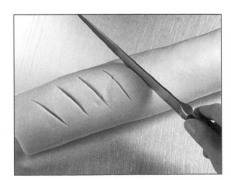

Using a sharp knife, slash the loaf diagonally at intervals.

ZUCCHINI AND OLIVE BREAD

Preparation time: 10 minutes
Total cooking time: 40 minutes
Serves 6–80

1 cup (135 g/4½ oz) finely grated
   zucchini
2 cups (250 g/8 oz) self-raising flour
1 teaspoon baking powder
1 teaspoon salt
1 teaspoon caster sugar
1 cup (125 g/4 oz) grated Cheddar
2 tablespoons chopped chives

12 pitted black olives, sliced
2 eggs
1 cup (250 ml/8 fl oz) milk
3 tablespoons olive oil

1 Preheat the oven to moderately hot 200°C (400°F/Gas 6). Generously grease one 20 x 10 cm (8 x 4 inch) loaf tin.
2 Squeeze as much moisture from the zucchini as possible and set aside.
3 In a large bowl sift the flour, baking powder, salt and sugar. Add the Cheddar, chives and olives. Beat the eggs and add the milk, oil and the zucchini and combine. Make a well in the centre of the dry

ingredients and add the zucchini mixture. Stir for 30 seconds, or until well combined.
4 Pour into the prepared tin and bake for 35–40 minutes, or until a skewer inserted comes out clean. Leave to rest for 5 minutes, then turn out onto a wire rack to cool.

COOK'S FILE
Hint: The best olives to use are Spanish as Kalamata olives taste a little bitter when cooked.

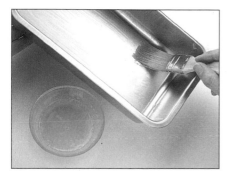

Generously grease the loaf tin with melted butter or oil.

Squeeze the excess moisture from the zucchini over a bowl or the kitchen sink.

Mix in the grated Cheddar, chives and olives to the flour mixture.

RICOTTA AND DILL BUNS

Preparation time: 20 minutes
+ 1 hour 40 minutes rising
Total cooking time: 45 minutes
Makes 8 buns

7 g (¼ oz) dried yeast
1½ tablespoons caster sugar
250 g (8 oz) ricotta cheese
30 g (1 oz) butter, softened
¼ small onion, grated
¼ teaspoon bicarbonate of soda
1 egg
3¾ cups (465 g/14½ oz) plain flour
2 tablespoons chopped dill

1 Mix together the yeast, sugar and ¼ cup (60 ml/2 fl oz) of warm water in a bowl. Cover the bowl and set aside in a warm place for 10 minutes, or until frothy.
2 Put the ricotta, butter, onion, bicarbonate of soda and egg in a food processor with 1 teaspoon of salt and process until smooth. Add the frothy yeast and 3 cups (375 g/12 oz) of the flour. Add the remaining flour and mix to a smooth dough. Turn out the dough onto a floured surface and knead for 6–8 minutes, or until smooth. Add the dill during the last minute of kneading.
3 Put in an oiled bowl, cover loosely with greased plastic wrap and set aside for 1 hour, or until doubled in size. Lightly grease one 20 x 30 cm (8 x 12 inch) tray.
4 Punch down the dough and divide into 8 pieces. Form into rounds and lay on the tray. Make 2 slashes on each bun. Cover with a damp tea towel for 30 minutes, or until well risen.
5 Preheat the oven to moderate 180°C (350°F/Gas 4). Bake the buns for 40–45 minutes, or until golden. Check after 20 minutes and reduce the oven to warm 170°C (325°F/ Gas 3) if they are too brown.

Scrape down the sides of the bowl and process the ricotta mixture until smooth.

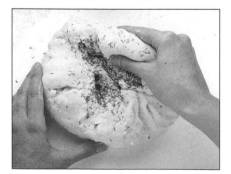

Knead the chopped dill into the dough during the last minute of kneading.

Using a sharp knife, slash the top of each bun twice.

Cut the egg yolks into the dry ingredients with a knife.

Put the raisins in a bowl, pour over the orange juice and leave to soften.

Divide the dough in half to make it easier to handle. Cut out rounds with a cutter.

Place the filling in the centre of the pastry round and then fold over to enclose.

FRUITY NUT PASTRIES

Preparation time: 1 hour + chilling
Total cooking time: 20 minutes
Makes 40

2½ cups (310 g/9¾ oz) plain flour
165 g (5½ oz) butter, chopped
½ cup (125 g/4 oz) caster sugar
2 eggs plus 1 yolk, beaten
2 teaspoons lemon juice
1 egg yolk, lightly beaten, extra
1 tablespoon demerara sugar

FRUIT AND NUT FILLING
125 g (4 oz) dried figs
75 g (2½ oz) raisins
2 tablespoons fresh orange juice
75 g (2½ oz) walnuts, finely chopped
100 g (3⅓ oz) blanched, roasted
   almonds, finely chopped
2 tablespoons marmalade
1½ tablespoons grated orange rind
¼ teaspoon ground cloves
1 teaspoon ground cinnamon

1 Sift the flour into a bowl and rub in the butter with your fingertips. Stir through the sugar, then add the eggs and yolk and cut through with a knife to combine; add enough lemon juice to form a dough. Gather together into a ball, cover with plastic wrap and refrigerate for about 30 minutes.
2 To make Fruit and Nut Filling: Chop the figs, cover with boiling water and leave for 15 minutes to soften. Put the raisins in a bowl, cover with orange juice and leave for 15 minutes to soften. Drain the figs and raisins and combine in a bowl with the remaining filling ingredients.
3 Preheat the oven to moderate 180°C (350°F/Gas 4). Cut the dough in half to make it easier to work with. Roll out each half to about 5 mm (¼ inch) thick on a lightly floured surface and cut rounds, using an 8 cm (3 inch) cutter. Spoon 1 full teaspoon of filling into the centre of each round, brush the edges lightly with water and fold over to enclose the filling.
4 Place on a lightly greased oven tray, brush with extra egg yolk and sprinkle with demerara sugar. Make cuts across the top of each pastry. Repeat with the remaining dough and filling. Bake for 20 minutes, or until lightly browned.

197

BISCUITS

FLORENTINES

Preheat the oven to moderate 180°C (350°F/Gas 4). Line an oven tray with baking paper. Sift ¼ cup (30 g/1 oz) plain flour into a bowl. Add 2 tablespoons each of chopped walnuts, chopped flaked almonds, finely chopped glacé cherries and finely chopped mixed peel and stir to combine. Combine 75 g (2½ oz) butter and ¼ cup (45 g/1½ oz) soft brown sugar in a pan, stirring over low heat until the butter has melted and the sugar dissolved. Add to the bowl and mix until just combined. Drop heaped teaspoonsful of the mixture onto the tray, leaving about 6 cm (2½ inches) between each. Press into neat 5 cm (2 inch) rounds. Bake for 7 minutes, then cool on the tray for 5 minutes. Lift carefully onto a wire rack to allow to cool completely. Repeat with the remaining mixture. Spread one side of each Florentine with melted dark chocolate and leave until set. Makes 24.

PANFORTE

Preheat the oven to moderate 180°C (350°F/Gas 4). Brush a 20 cm (8 inch) round cake tin with oil or melted butter and line the base with baking paper. Combine ⅔ cup (90 g/3 oz) each of slivered almonds, chopped macadamia nuts and chopped walnuts in a large bowl with 1½ cups (285 g/9¼ oz) mixed dried fruit. Sift together ⅔ cup (85 g/2¾ oz) plain flour, 2 tablespoons cocoa powder and 1 teaspoon ground cinnamon and add to the bowl. Stir 60 g (2 oz) butter, 60 g (2 oz) chopped dark chocolate, ⅓ cup (90 g/3 oz) caster sugar and ¼ cup (90 g/3 oz) honey together in a small pan over low heat until melted and combined. Add to the dry ingredients and stir until just combined. Spoon into the tin and smooth the surface. Bake in the preheated oven for 50 minutes and then leave to cool completely in the tin before turning out. Dust with icing sugar and cut into thin wedges to serve. Makes 25 wedges.

Biscuits from left: Florentines; Panforte; Chocolate Wafers; Biscotti; Amaretti

BISCOTTI

Preheat the oven to warm 160°C (315°F/Gas 2–3). Lighly oil a large oven tray and line with baking paper. Beat 3 eggs, 1 cup (250 g/8 oz) caster sugar and 1 teaspoon vanilla essence with electric beaters for 2 minutes, or until light and frothy. Sift in 2½ cups (310 g/9¾ oz) plain flour, ½ cup (60 g/2 oz) self-raising flour, 1 teaspoon bicarbonate of soda and a pinch of salt and add ¾ cup (115 g/3¾ oz) toasted almonds. Mix with a knife to a soft dough. Divide into 3 portions and roll into log shapes about 20 cm (8 inches) long. Place on the tray and bake for 50 minutes. Cool on a wire rack. Cut the logs into thin slices, place on the tray and bake for 8 minutes each side. Cool and serve. Makes 50.

CHOCOLATE WAFERS

Preheat the oven to slow 150°C (300°F/Gas 2) and line 3 oven trays with baking paper. Finely chop ⅔ cup (100 g/3⅓ oz) almonds. Finely chop 100 g (3⅓ oz) dark chocolate and add to the almonds with ½ teaspoon each of finely grated orange and lemon rind. Beat 2 egg whites with a pinch of salt until soft peaks form. Gradually add ½ cup icing sugar, beating well after each addition, until thick and glossy. Fold gently into the nut mixture. Place heaped teaspoonsful of the mixture on the trays and spread into 5 cm (2 inch) rounds. Bake for 20 minutes, until crisp and lightly coloured. Cool on the trays. Makes 30.

AMARETTI

Line 2 baking trays with baking paper. Finely grind 125 g (4 oz) blanched almonds in a food processor and then mix in a bowl with ½ cup (125 g/4 oz) caster sugar. Whisk an egg white until frothy and add almost all to the almond mixture; stir to form a dough that is stiff, but soft enough to pipe (add more of the egg white if necessary). Spoon the mixture into a piping bag with a large nozzle and pipe small discs a little apart on the trays. Sift over a little icing sugar and press an almond into the centre of each. Leave, uncovered, for 4 hours at room temperature. Preheat the oven to slow 150°C (300°F/Gas 2). Bake for 25 minutes, or until lightly browned, and then cool on the trays. Makes about 35.

CITRUS ALMOND BISCUITS

Preparation time: 15 minutes
+ 20 minutes refrigeration
Total cooking time:
12–15 minutes
Makes 30

60 g butter
½ teaspoon grated orange rind
½ teaspoon grated lime rind
¼ cup caster sugar
½ cup plain flour

2 tablespoons ground almonds
1 egg white
1 cup flaked almonds, crushed
icing sugar

1 Line an oven tray with baking paper. Preheat the oven to moderate 180°C. Place the butter, orange rind, lime rind and sugar in a small mixing bowl. Using electric beaters, beat until light and creamy.
2 Add the flour and ground almonds and mix with a flat-bladed knife to a soft dough. Press mixture with hands until it comes together.

3 Roll teaspoonsful of the mixture into 2 cm-long logs. Refrigerate for 20 minutes or until mixture is firm. Lightly whisk the egg white with a fork. Lightly crush the almonds with your hands. Place in a small bowl. Dip each log into egg white, roll in almonds then place on the prepared tray. Bake in a preheated oven for 12–15 minutes or until lightly golden. Dust with icing sugar while still warm. Allow to cool on tray.

COOK'S FILE
Storage time: Store in airtight container for up to 3 weeks.

1

2

3

CHOCOLATE ALMOND TARTS

Preparation time: 40 minutes
Total cooking time: 20 minutes
Makes 18

1 cup plain flour
pinch salt
60 g butter, chopped
1 tablespoon icing sugar
1 tablespoon lemon juice

FILLING
1 egg
⅓ cup caster sugar
2 tablespoons cocoa
½ cup ground almonds
3 tablespoons cream
¼ cup apricot jam
18 blanched almonds

1 Preheat oven to moderate 180°C. Brush two shallow patty cake tins with melted butter or oil. Process flour, salt, butter and icing sugar in food processor, using pulse action, 10 seconds or until fine crumbs form. Add juice, process until mixture forms a ball. Roll between sheets of waxed paper to 6 mm thickness. Cut into 7-cm rounds with fluted cutter. Place in tins, refrigerate 20 minutes.
2 To make the Filling: Using electric beaters, beat egg and sugar until thick and pale. Sift cocoa on top. With flat-bladed knife, stir in almonds and cream.
3 Place a dab of jam in centre of each tart. Spoon filling into tarts, place an almond in centre. Bake 15 minutes or until puffed and set on top. Leave in tins 5 minutes then cool on wire racks. Dust with icing sugar if desired.

MIXED NUT BISCOTTI

Preparation time: 30 minutes
Total cooking time: 45 minutes
Makes about 50

25 g almonds
25 g hazelnuts
75 g unsalted pistachios
3 egg whites
½ cup caster sugar
¾ cup plain flour

1 Preheat the oven to moderate 180°C. Brush a 26 x 8 x 4.5 cm bar tin with oil or melted butter, then line base and sides with baking paper. Spread the almonds, hazelnuts and pistachios onto a flat baking tray and place in oven for 2–3 minutes, until nuts are just toasted; cool. Place the egg whites in a small, clean, dry mixing bowl. Using electric beaters, beat egg whites until stiff peaks form. Add the sugar gradually, beating constantly until the mixture is thick and glossy and all the sugar has dissolved.

2 Transfer mixture to a large mixing bowl. Add sifted flour and nuts. Using a metal spoon, gently fold ingredients together until combined. Spread into prepared tin and smooth the surface. Bake for 25 minutes; remove from oven and cool completely in tin.

3 Preheat the oven to moderately slow 160°C. Using a sharp, serrated knife, cut the baked loaf into 5 mm slices. Spread slices onto oven trays and bake for about 15 minutes, turning once halfway through cooking, until the slices are lightly golden and crisp. Serve Mixed Nut Biscotti to dip into coffee, or with a sweet dessert wine.

COOK'S FILE
Storage time: Mixed Nut Biscotti will keep for up to a week in an airtight container.

CHOC-DIPPED MACAROONS

Preparation time: 25 minutes
Total cooking time: 15 minutes
Makes about 24

1 egg white
⅓ cup caster sugar
2 teaspoons cornflour
1 cup dessicated coconut
65 g dark compound
    chocolate

1 Preheat oven to moderately slow 160°C. Line a biscuit tray with baking paper. Place the egg white in a small, dry mixing bowl. Using electric beaters, beat until firm peaks form. Add the sugar gradually, beating constantly until the mixture is thick and glossy and all the sugar has dissolved. Add the cornflour and beat until ingredients are just combined.

2 Add the coconut to the egg white mixture. Using a metal spoon, stir until just combined. Roll heaped teaspoons of the mixture into balls and place on the prepared tray. Bake for 15–20 minutes until macaroons are lightly golden. Remove from the oven and leave to cool on the tray.

3 Place the chocolate in a small bowl over a pan of barely simmering water. When the chocolate is beginning to soften, stir until it is smooth. Dip the tops of the macaroons into the melted chocolate and allow the excess to drain. Place the macaroons on a foil-lined tray and leave to set.

COOK'S FILE
Storage time: Store in an airtight container for up to a day. Hint: Use to accompany a soft, creamy dessert.

*Mixed Nut Biscotti (top)
and Choc-Dipped Macaroons*

INDEX

USEFUL INFORMATION

All our recipes are thoroughly tested. Standard metric measuring cups and spoons are used in the development of our recipes. All cup and spoon measurements are level. We have used 60 g eggs in all recipes. Sizes of cans vary from manufacturer to manufacturer and between countries—use the can size closest to the one suggested in the recipe.

CONVERSION GUIDE

1 cup	= 250 ml (8 fl oz)
1 teaspoon	= 5 ml
1 Australian tablespoon	= 20 ml (4 teaspoons)
1 UK/US tablespoon	= 15 ml (3 teaspoons)

Dry Measures	Liquid Measures	Linear Measures
30 g = 1 oz	30 ml = 1 fl oz	6 mm = ¼ inch
250 g = 8 oz	125 ml = 4 fl oz	1 cm = ½ inch
500 g = 1 lb	250 ml = 8 fl oz	2.5 cm = 1 inch

CUP CONVERSIONS—DRY INGREDIENTS

1 cup almonds, slivered	= 125 g (4 oz)
whole	= 155 g (5 oz)
1 cup cheese, lightly packed	= 125 g (4 oz)
processed cheddar	= 155 g (5 oz)
1 cup flour, plain, or self-raising	= 125 g (4 oz)
wholemeal	= 140 g (4½ oz)
1 cup minced beef or pork	= 250 g (8 oz)
1 cup pasta shapes	= 125 g (4 oz)
1 cup raisins	= 170 g (5½ oz)
1 cup rice, short grain, raw	= 200 g (6½ oz)
1 cup sesame seeds	= 160 g (5 oz)
1 cup split peas	= 250 g (8 oz)

OVEN TEMPERATURES

Where temperature ranges are indicated, the lower figure applies to gas ovens, the higher to electric ovens. This allows for the fact that the flame in gas ovens generates a drier heat, which effectively cooks food faster than the moister heat of an electric oven, even if the temperature setting is the same.

	°C	°F	Gas Mark
Very slow	120	250	fi
Slow	150	300	2
Mod slow	160	325	3
Moderate	180	350	4
Mod hot	190(g) – 210(e)	375 – 425	5
Hot	200(g) – 240(e)	400 – 475	6
Very hot	230(g) – 260(e)	450 – 525	8

(g) = gas (e) = electric

Note: For fan-forced ovens, check your appliance manual, but as a general rule, set the oven temperature to 20°C lower than the temperature indicated in the recipe.

INTERNATIONAL GLOSSARY

capsicum	sweet bell pepper
chick pea	garbanzo bean
cornflour	cornstarch
eggplant	aubergine
plain flour	all-purpose flour
spring onion	scallion
zucchini	courgette

First published 2003 by Murdoch Books Ltd, Ferry House, 51–57 Lacy Road, Putney, London SW15 1PR, UK.
This edition published 2003 for Index Books Ltd, Henson Way, Kettering, NN16 8PX, UK

ISBN 1 740453 17 4
A catalogue record for this book is available from the British library

Managing Editor: Anna Cheifetz **Design Manager:** Helen Taylor
Chief Executive: Juliet Rogers **Production Manager:** Lucy Byrne
Colour separation by Colourscan, Singapore **Printed** in Slovenia